Praise for *Out of M*

"Like a stack of photo[...] [...]er life
growing up in Californi[...] prose
and keen observations, [...] [...]se of humor.
Here is how one determ[...] [...]an made her way home
while finding the love of her life—loving herself. In the end,
Meredith will show you that all you have to do is step out of
your shoes."
—Jay Gilbertson, Author of *Moon Over Madeline Island*

"Good writing enables readers to empathize, to see parts of
their own lives in what the writer is saying. I read this memoir
in one sitting because I couldn't put it down. It was a joy from
start to finish."
—Sandy Little, Editor

"Wonderfully readable. Reflective, poignant and humorous
stories about family, friends and re-envisioned environments.
We come away from this book smiling and refreshed."
—Ellen and George Anthonisen, Bucks County, PA

"*Out of My Shoes* is a lyrical and unsparing testimony of one
woman's emergence from a sheltered fifties girlhood through
marriage and motherhood to an unexpected awakening.
Meredith Stout has a keen ear for the nuances of social
hierarchy and the gratifying thunder of social change. Shot
through with humor, anger and love, *Out of My Shoes* is a
lively companion for anyone desiring to take a road trip with a
woman determined to encounter a larger world. "
—Alison Luterman, Author, *In the Time of Great Fires*

Out of My Shoes

A MEMOIR

by Meredith Stout

For Ellynore, with love and gratitude for our years of creativity and friendship,

Meredith

Merry Death

For
Cam, Jenny and Kate,
who are always there for me

And for Zelma

"Remember only this one thing," said Badger.
"The stories people tell have a way of taking care of them. If stories come to you, care for them and learn to give them away when they are needed. Sometimes a person needs a story more than food to stay alive. That is why we put these stories in each other's memories. This is how people care for themselves."

—Barry Lopez, *Crow and Weasel*

Book design: Irene Rietschel
Cover design: Marion Riggs
Technical assistance: Ruth Cox

Image credits:
Cover photograph by the author's father, Charlton M. Lewis, Jr.
Photograph of the author by Katherine Briccetti Photography
Back cover photography by Charlton M. Lewis, Jr., the late Betty McAfee, Meredith Stout

Poetry by the late Zelma Brown appears with permission of Mark and Matthew Brown.
Down In the River to Pray attributed to George H. Allan, Slave Songbook of 1867.

ISBN: 978-0-9905894-3-3

Printed with Lulu.com in the US

Table of Contents

Author's Note

I have changed the names of most, though not all the individuals in *Out of My Shoes* in order to protect their privacy. While the dialogue, with some exceptions, is necessarily paraphrased, it is nonetheless true to the meaning and emotional content of what was said at the time. In some cases, I rearranged the chronology and sequence of events, but not the events themselves. Several of the stories in *Out of My Shoes* were included in the anthology, *A Basket of Words*, published together with Theo Cavanaugh and Ruth Cox in 2014. Photographs are not included in the book, but are available on my website, www.meredithstout.com.

A Kind of a Prologue

"So, girlfriend, what's a nice lady like you doing road tripping around the country with a big ol' black lesbian like me?" Jayda's androgynous bulk under a baseball cap and wrap-around sunglasses beside me in my station wagon made her look like a cross between a complacent Buddha and a Hells Angel. She turned to grin at me, and her hair, dyed a startling sunflower gold, contrasted with skin darkened to a deeper bronze from the sun. Her vast T-shirt almost touched the steering wheel, and her legs, in their Nikes, protruded from knee-length royal blue shorts like oak trees. My own legs stretched long below a preppy J. Crew polo shirt, shorts and sandals; our elbows touched casually on the armrest between us, while the summer wind blew hot across our cheeks.

At the end of every spring, I get wandering feet. Distant highways beckon me to roll down the windows, turn on the cruise control, and dial up the tunes. It had been my idea to take Jayda on a road trip that first carefree summer before the millennium. Our lives moved on such different paths, mine in Berkeley, hers in Vallejo. Chaos followed her wherever she went—crises with family, bouts of depression, and the endless unpredictability that comes from having no money or safety net. I lived secure in my own home where I had a steady income, a college diploma and a darkroom where I liked to work.

At the age of thirty-seven, Jayda was twenty-five years younger than me, and I wanted to give her a treat, show her new places, and introduce her to national parks where she'd never been. It felt exciting to road trip with her, a black woman, to see the country through her curiosity about everything around her, and to have these weeks with her alone. I liked her voluminous physicality, the way her eyes crinkled half shut when she laughed, the way she hugged me and made me feel loved.

"Because I thought it would be fun," I said finally.

"That's what I think too." She laughed her comforting big belly laugh and gave me a high five.

I have always believed that if I only worked hard enough, there would be, at some point, an "Aha" moment that would hold the solution to life's questions. But the older I get, the less time I spend looking for elusive answers I can never find. Instead, memories surface, sometimes slowly, like images emerging from a darkroom's developing pan. Other times, they spring, often unexpectedly, out of hidden recesses in my mind. Almost forgotten stories unfold out of those photographs as if a video that had been frozen in midstream suddenly began to play.

It is true I have no solutions, but I can write those stories. And, in their telling, I watch themes weave into a pattern that gives me a better understanding of what my life has been about. I want to tell you more about Jayda, but there are other stories that I need to tell first.

Some Fundamental Contradictions

When I was no more than five, Gertrude drove an old Model-A Ford to our house once a week to do the laundry. I liked to sneak behind the kitchen door to watch her crank dripping sheets through mangle rollers on our screened-in back porch. Tall and silent, Gertrude paid no attention to me as her ropey arms strained to work the heavy load.

Whenever I tiptoed across the porch to our backyard, I stole a sideways look at the inside of her hands. During those early war years, we lived in a white neighborhood in Pasadena, and she was the first "colored" woman I had seen up close. The pinkness of her palms, creased with lines of brown, surprised me and I wondered if there were other parts of her body that were pink. Did she have sharp lines like our bathing suit tans after summers at the beach? Mother always said the sun was good for us and we should be "brown as berries" before we went back to school.

When the war was over in 1945, my family left Pasadena and Gertrude behind to move to a new home in the countryside of Altadena only a few blocks from the San Gabriel Mountains. My older brother Thad was fifteen, my sister Annie eleven, and I was nine. The rambling, pine-encircled house, with its backyard of delicious smelling fruit trees and tangles of vines looked larger than it was because it was a split-level, with an added wing that gave it the shape of an L. It was built on a slope. To my young eyes, it was very grand. Stairs led from the kitchen down to two bedrooms that Annie and I took over on the lower floor, and from Annie's room, a door through a laundry opened to a patio with an impressive stone fireplace. Surrounded by open fields, but shielded behind a vine-covered fence, the house was across the street from a county park, with two tired tennis courts and a baseball field. There was even a shed-like stable at the end of our yard where Annie and I kept our horses, Buster and fat old Willy, with his one blue eye and one brown. Mother painted the house number a dark green on the tilted mailbox outside the gate, and till the end of time, we would refer to our home simply as 596.

My family always had various household help. After we moved in, Mother hired a "colored" man who wore torn khaki pants to do the heavy work on our acre of land. His name was Proctor, not Mister Anybody, just Proctor. Like Rochester on Jack Benny's radio program, I didn't know if it was his first or last name. I didn't notice that no one brought him a sandwich, or that he drank water out of a garden hose. I never thought about how he got to our house at the top of the hill or how he made his way home.

When I turned eleven, I was old enough to see the movie, *Gone with the Wind*. After that, I began to worry that people might think our white house in its neighborhood of smaller houses might look like a Southern plantation with the big wooden gate Dad had built in front and with Proctor working in the back. If by accident our eyes met on my way to the horses, I gave him an embarrassed little wave and looked the other way. Without my knowing, the image of his figure moving among the citrus trees quietly worked its way into my heart.

Our part-time housekeeper wasn't at all like Proctor or lanky Gertrude. Mrs. Black was white. Three times a week, Mother drove down Lake Street to meet her bus at the bottom of the hill. Solidly overweight, she sat at the kitchen table taking a full hour to eat her breakfast after we had finished ours, smacking her lips with a satisfied "mmhm umhm" over fried eggs, toast and the jellied pigs' feet she kept in a bowl in the back of our icebox. After a while, she became so much a part of our family that, with the exception of my father, we lapsed into the habit of calling her Auntie B. But Dad, raised in a large Victorian house in New Haven with several Irish maids, never failed to address her by anything but the formal "Mrs. Black."

Annie and I loved it when Mother let us go by bus with Auntie B to the horse races at the Santa Anita racetrack. While she placed her $2 bets, we leaned against the rails and mooned over the horses with adolescent devotion. She told us stories that fed my growing fascination with people who were different from us. Like when she told us about bus trips to Reno with her sister, Coco, where they played the one-armed bandits, and how Coco laundered their dollar bills and hung them on the line to dry after they came home. I don't believe Auntie B had a shred of self-consciousness in her ample soul. She told us that when she wanted to take a plane to visit her son Alan in Chicago, she had to buy a second seat to support the width of her behind. To earn the extra money, she got herself on a Hollywood variety radio show and delighted the audience with her enthusiastic rendition of "Has Anybody Here Seen Kelly?"

When Auntie B went into a rest home with a stroke, May, a light-skinned "Negro" woman, came every week to clean. Wiry and hardworking, May had recently moved to Altadena from the South. "How you doing, Missus Lewis?" she always asked my mother after she had put her bag in the same place on the bed in the guest room.

"Hello, May, thank you, I'm doing fine. How's your mother?" May's mother was sick with cancer, and I knew she had to work extra hard to pay the bills. Mother went out of her way to be friendly to May, but once when I was home from college, she told me that she put her own purse in her bottom bureau drawer on the mornings May was there.

"Mom! You don't really think May would take money from your purse?"

"Certainly not!" Mother was incensed. "It's not that I don't trust May, but you know how badly she needs money. When there isn't any temptation, it's easier for everyone." I never got used to my mother's curious combination of warmly generous hospitality mixed with an engrained Victorian snobbism.

My best friend, freckle-nosed Peggy, lived with her sister and two brothers in a crowded little house down the street. Her family kept horses too, and, with pigtails bouncing, we imagined we were cowboys as we ripped along open trails carved against the hills past flowering oleander and spiking yucca plants. But I knew Peggy's family was different from mine. They had no hired help, her father sold vacuum cleaners, and their dog from the pound was appropriately named Rags. My own father was a scientist with a Ph.D. from Caltech, and our large pedigreed poodles sported ridiculously upright pompoms for tails. Mother was casually friendly with Peggy's mother, but it would never have occurred to my parents to invite them for a family meal. The summer after I turned twelve, I was sure my heart was broken forever when Peggy's family moved away.

Duct Tape

I was never sure if we had enough money or not. It was confusing to see my usually cheerful mother, her brow knitted and her cigarette smoldering in an ashtray nearby, thumbing through her checkbook next to a collection of bills. Once I overheard my parents in the kitchen worrying about my father's salary at the small firm where he researched scientific patents. When Mother chided him for not charging clients more, he said he didn't think he had worked hard enough to charge a higher fee. How do you know when you've worked hard enough, I wondered. How do you know when you're safe? Maybe my grandmother in New Haven helped pay the bills.

Mother's father had been in a cotton business that lost everything in the Depression, a man and an event I knew little about and that seemed very long ago. She didn't talk about it much, but we rarely bought anything new. It was simply the way we lived. If something broke, Mother fixed it with duct tape. Behind her chair, a potholder lay next to a lamp with a broken switch. "Do not move this potholder," read a sign in her emphatic scrawl, "It turns the light bulb on and off." Our ailing washing machine was nearly dead before she agreed to buy a new one, and one of those new-fangled clothes dryers must have been a luxury beyond our means. I worried about poor Auntie B who had to haul herself and a laundry hamper down a rutted path to the wire clothesline in the back, but the sweet scent of sun-dried sheets on a freshly made bed was one of the pleasures of our daily life.

Whenever we went out to dinner, which was rare, I knew better than to choose anything above a certain price. A hamburger for 75 cents was all right, but I could only look longingly at the juicy looking ham dinner with pineapple that cost twice as much. This habit of frugality became so engrained that to this day I mechanically check the price of every item on a menu. After I left for college, a musty-smelling house trailer joined the family, perhaps in an effort to fill the empty nest. Mother christened her "Waltzing Matilda," which delighted me and gave the old trailer an aura of magic and feminine identity she didn't deserve. Mother spiffed her up with plaid window curtains, and when my parents weren't taking her on a winter foray to a desert campground, Waltzing Matilda spent her time next to the driveway collecting sap from one of the dripping pine trees.

By contrast, Mother made sure that our Christmases were luxuriously abundant affairs. Throughout the fall, I could hardly bear the excitement watching a mound of wrapped presents hidden on her closet shelf gradually expand. Christmas eve had nothing to do with the birth of the holy baby Jesus Christ and everything to do with hanging stockings, putting out cookies for Santa, and reciting *The Night Before Christmas*. On Christmas Day, there seemed to be no end to the presents and the ritual of opening one gift at a time could take the entire day. Of course every scrap of decorative paper and ribbon was saved for the following year.

Another contradiction to Mother's concern about imminent poverty was when we installed a backyard swimming pool. We were astonished when Cousin Anna, a long-forgotten relative who lived somewhere far away, conveniently died and left Mother the astronomical sum of two thousand dollars. Rather than putting the money for safekeeping in a bank, she immediately hired workmen to dig a hole in the backyard and line it with cement. My sister Annie and I resented having to give up spring weekends to help Dad lay tile and the flagstone deck with his usual passion for geometric precision. Nonetheless, we learned what was involved in building a pool, and when it was finished, it became a focus of our lives. On soft August nights,

I sometimes stripped naked to slide into silken water as warm as the night around me, float on my back, and watch the light in my parents' room click off while crickets sang their summer song.

Whether we could afford it or not, it was understood that our family would never belong to the Altadena Country Club. "That's what fancy people do," Mother said with a note of scorn whenever we drove by. Looking wistfully, if a bit shyly, at the tree-shaded club house and fenced tennis courts, I wondered if there was something wrong with having money. By contrast, during the war years, we spent blissful summer weeks in a campground where we children ran free as sandpipers on a Southern California beach. Dad constructed our makeshift "house" out of two strong-smelling Army surplus tents for bedrooms connected by a canvas-covered wood frame that housed a table, chairs and a two-burner stove. An orange-crated entertainment center was complete with a portable radio, board games and books. The nearby ocean was our playground, our shower and our tub. Who could want for anything more?

The Grunion Run in the middle of every August was always the best. One summer, the year I turned eight, we ran blinking from the lighted cabin after dinner into the black of the beach, plastic buckets bumping against our shins. The moon's path stretched from the horizon, and bonfires like Fourth of July sparklers dotted the sand. Chasing about in the soft sand in search of the silvery fish, we half stumbled as waves rose unseen from the inky ocean before exploding with a warm rush against our legs. Ahead of me, I could see my older brother Thad and sister Annie grabbing at grunion with their bare hands. Determined to keep up, I scanned each line of foam for glints of the fish as they danced out of the shallows to lay their eggs, only to watch them vanish again into bubbling white. Thad stopped to show me four fish slapping feebly in the bottom of his bucket. "Not fair," I complained, holding out my empty bucket. "You and Annie always win."

The moon grew dimmer as the evening waned, and it was time to go back. We showed the fish to Mother, their scales shining in the cabin's light. "I know they're fun to catch, but they're much too small to eat," she said. "Will one of you please throw them in the garbage tomorrow before they begin to smell."

The next morning, the pail on the back porch made a spot of yellow against the flat grey light. Because it was Thad and Annie's turn to wash up the breakfast dishes, it fell to me to deal with the fish. "If I were a grunion," I said to the bucket, "I wouldn't want to end up in the garbage." I carried the pail up a narrow trail to the top of the cliff behind the cabin where, beneath the morning fog, I could see to the end of the cove across the cottage roofs.

How do you pray for fish, I wondered, as I gingerly picked up each fish by its tail and laid it in the hole I had dug with a stick among the ice plants. "I'm glad I didn't catch you," I told them as I covered them with sandy dirt. I decorated the grave with four magenta flowers, and scratched "Poor Fish" across the top. The only religious words I knew were from a psalm that Sally Smith who lived across the street at home had taught me. She told me if I tore a page in the Bible I'd go to Hell. I don't think I've opened one since. "The Lord is My Shepherd, I walk beside green pastures," I intoned solemnly. That didn't seem adequate, so I said it twice. Finally, feeling a little silly, I patted the grave in a last farewell, and slid down the path, shovel, bucket and all, just as the sun began to shine, a giant white globe behind the morning mist.

Early Academia

For my parents, intellectual sophistication, rather than financial status or religious involvement, was the yardstick by which they lived. Radio commentator Howard K. Smith was their Sunday morning church, the *New York Times* was their bible, and Franklin Delano Roosevelt was God. As faithfully as any religion, they attended a monthly "Deep Thinkers Club," where I guess they talked deep thoughts. Or rather, the wives listened while their husbands talked.

Mother did her pontificating at home. I can still see her holding court from her chair in the corner of the study, a Webster's Dictionary on the bookshelf next to her, along with a beginning Spanish language text, and "A Short History of the Russian People" that I never saw her read. "Oh, my God! Those damn Republicans!" She peers around the paper to fix her pale blue eyes on my father. "How could they!" Dad looks up patiently from a new biography of Adlai Stevenson, marks the page with the flat of his hand, and after a thoughtfully considered comment or two of his own, goes quietly back to his book.

Their friends were primarily scientists—nuclear physicists at Cal Tech, or researchers at the nearby Jet Propulsion Lab. Some had even worked in New Mexico developing the atomic bomb; all of them considered themselves to be liberal Democrats like my parents, and not one of them was black. We children were raised to call these prominent academics and their wives by their first names, a deliberate emphasis on informal western living that seemed entirely natural to us.

Mother and Dad were raised on the East Coast, and I grew up in a family steeped in the Ivy League tradition. The men all went to Yale, where my grandfather had been revered as a prominent professor of English. My aunts went to Vassar, though one left to study violin in Italy, an unimaginable act of courage to my young mind. My mother went to Smith. Of course, women were supposed to go to college, but it was to prepare them to marry educated men, not to train them for a career. Nothing was defined in so many words; it was simply in the air we breathed. When Thad was sent to Thatcher, a prestigious prep school in the Ojai Valley, it was assumed that Annie and I would stay home to go to local public schools. "We had a choice between keeping horses for you girls or sending you to private school," Mother always said. "Aren't you glad we chose horses?"

"Yes," we chorused, and at first, that suited me just fine. Being home in my early adolescence felt safe. I was younger than my classmates and plagued by bouts of anxiety that I wouldn't be able to keep up. Not that our schools, large and loosely discipined with a limited curriculum, were particularly difficult compared to rigorous private schools. In an eighth grade English class, any love of Shakespeare was crushed as we labored through a reading of *The Merchant of Venice*; in high school, my math classes didn't go beyond geometry, and the French teacher had never been to France.

Intellectual curiosity, the backbone of my parents' life, had never been my strongest suit. At an early age, I longed for babies of my own. I played with a life-size doll with real baby furniture well beyond what would be considered normal for a girl in her pre-teens. A book entitled *Room for One More* about wise, all-knowing parents who adopted disabled children they raised into blooming health along with their own, held my adolescent attention for years. I must have read the book at least six times. I never questioned Mother's definition of a mother as the one in the family who chose the rotten peach. That's what I want to be, I thought, a competent wife and mother whose children are happy and safe.

But my personal appearance consumed me the most. I absorbed every issue of *Calling All Girls* and *Seventeen* for advice on makeup, clothes and how to be appealing to young men. One of Mother's Betty Crocker cookbooks even had suggestions: "Apply makeup every morning to raise your family's spirits." "Bake cookies while washing dishes," or "Be interested in your husband—and you'll always be interesting to him."

During my senior year of high school, a wealthy relative came into my life. My father's Aunt Alice, a devoted Vassar College alumna and a mythical figure to me, had offered to pay the tuition of any young woman in the family aspiring to attend her alma mater. There seemed to be no end of largesse from distant female relatives. "Great Aunt Alice married money," said Mother succinctly, as if that explained it all.

My tomboy sister said, "No, thank you," to Great Aunt Alice's offer to pay for Vassar, and chose the University of Colorado instead. But when it was my turn, I was immediately drawn to the glossy photographs in the 1952 *Vassar Bulletin*. Pretty young women sat smiling at each other on dormitory steps or rode bicycles under stately trees scattered across spacious lawns. Wearing neatly belted skirts and cardigan sweaters, the students looked happily carefree, as if they belonged to a coveted other world. They were shiny girls; I wanted to be one of them.

My parents worried that at the tender age of sixteen, I was too young for college, especially so far away. "When you're through with high school, you should take another year of study at a private school in Pasadena," they said. But I was not to be deterred. It felt embarrassing to be going to another year of high school while my friends went off to college. Given my family's Ivy League background, this women's college two hours north of New York City was, to my mind, an exciting and natural choice. Eventually, I got my way, applied to Vassar, and to my surprise, was accepted. That there might be demanding classes, deadlines and exams never entered my head.

Hallowed Halls

The majestic Super Chief glided into Pasadena on a sleepily warm September morning, so hazy that the end of the train disappeared into a scrim of smog. We clustered on the platform to watch, Mother all brave and smiley in her cotton dress with its white Peter Pan collar, and Dad, methodical in his checked shirt and gabardine pants with his vice-like squeeze on my upper arm in his version of a hug. I was thrilled by the huge wheezing engine and by the porter who bowed slightly as he pulled out a footstool in front of the steep stairs, touched his cap and called me "Miss."

The prospect of a trip across the country was even more exciting than the prospect of going to Vassar. Undaunted by my young age and convinced I was the picture of sophistication in my tweed traveling suit and heels as high as I could stand, I could hardly believe this was happening to me. I pressed my nose to the thickly misted window to wave again and again at Mother and Dad, who waved resolutely back through clouds of metallic smelling steam. I had not yet comprehended that in the age before jet planes, I would only go home for Christmas vacation and the summer months.

My first cousin had been assigned to look after me as far as his home in Chicago. Dirk had been spending his summer vacation with my family and, like my brother, was six years my senior and a Yale graduate. He had a prominent pinkish nose and sagging eyes that were a caricature of my father, but with none of Dad's good looks. "Do you like baseball?" he asked before we'd been half an hour underway. Unlike anyone in my family, his primary interest in life was the Chicago White Sox. While deserts and prairies, wooden station buildings and back street towns rolled past, I listened to explanations of innings, hits and errors, batting averages and what team was winning what series and why. By the time we reached Chicago and my cousin said goodbye, baseball and the fatigue of sitting up for two nights had depleted whatever excitement in this adventure I once had. There was still an overnight train to navigate by myself from Chicago to New York. I was beginning to understand the enormity of what I had chosen to do.

"Taxi, lady?" I stood rooted in the middle of Penn Station, where travellers streamed in every direction, lights flashed, and announcements blared. A uniformed arm reached towards my feet, and to my dismay, a porter grabbed up my suitcase as if he owned it and took off through the crowd. There was nothing for it but to totter after him in my torturous heels, clutching the fifty-cent piece Mother had said would be enough tip. A revolving door loomed ahead. I had never seen a revolving door. Convinced that he and my suitcase would vanish into the city without me, I threw myself into the door, jamming myself into the same compartment as the porter and my suitcase. Our bodies bumped together and my chin nearly rested on his shoulder as I danced on tiptoe to keep from stepping on his heels. There was just time for him to turn once to roll his eyes at me in astonishment before the door spewed us both out the other side. I had landed in New York.

Waiting for me was a world I did not know. I have no memory of my visit in New York with an uncle and aunt, or the train trip up the Hudson River. But when the campus taxi drove through the stone entrance gate, I stared directly at Main Hall. There was nothing hospitable about that massive building with its formal porte-cochère and rows of small-paned windows that stared blankly back. Towering trees did their best to soften the austerity of nearby brick dormitories, but inside, the rooms opening off linoleum hallways with their clanging fire doors were devoid of charm. It was a relief to be met in Room 207 by my new roommate, Diane, who had arrived in the comforting company of her mother and one of her aunts. Later, we did what we could to make the metal beds look homey with plaid bedspreads from the campus thrift shop, but I never got used to the steam heat radiator, relentless as an alarm clock, that clanked on each morning before it was light.

The *Vassar Bulletin* hadn't mentioned that men were only allowed in dorm rooms in the afternoons, and that a uniformed matron, known as the White Angel, sat at the front door to monitor whoever came and went. Or that we were required to wear a skirt for dinner that was served so early it felt like the middle of the afternoon. I tried not to long for our cocktail hour at 596 where my parents read family letters aloud, and we ate supper on trays by the fire.

It was the college-level classes that undid my efforts to adjust. I forgot about being sophisticated as I peered into the abyss of what I didn't know. In Freshman English, our first paper was on "Chain Mail in Beowulf." I stared at the teacher in disbelief. Three to five pages on Old English armor? With footnotes? I looked around at other girls gathering up their books; they seemed unperturbed by this assignment. "What's a footnote?" I asked Diane, who tried to conceal her surprise at my ignorance as she gamely walked me through the mechanics of writing a college paper. But at the end of mid-terms, I was mortified to be put on academic probation for a D in English. Before our Thanksgiving break, I was required to keep an appointment with the Dean.

The door to her office was at the end of a drab corridor in Main Hall, where a brass plaque on the door read *Elizabeth Dorsett, Warden.* That the Dean of Students was called the Warden was a campus joke, but I had never expected to meet her face to face. She nodded me into a wooden armchair across the desk, her grey hair pulled back severely and secured by what might have been a knitting needle. With my hands clenched in my lap, I watched her glance through my collection of papers, sit back in her chair and look at me over her reading glasses. She cleared her throat.

"I don't know how you got in here," she said, not unkindly. Unable to meet her eyes, I looked past her through the small-paned window to the library tower and grey November sky with its promise of snow. "I got all A's in high school." My voice was whispery.

"My dear, everyone here gets A's in high school." We sat in silence while I tried to think of other ways I might have gotten in. I couldn't remember my scores on entrance exams; in fact, I barely remembered taking them. At last, I offered the information that my Great Aunt Alice, whom I had never met but who was funding my tuition, had gone to Vassar. "I think her last name is Martin. It used to be Robbins."

The Warden's eyebrows arched into semi-circles and then she nodded as if she had made a remarkable discovery of her own. "Ahhhh, now I see," she said with a slight smile. "Alice Robbins Martin is your great aunt." There was a long pause while I digested the idea that Vassar had accepted me because of my Aunt Alice's wealth. But Mrs. Dorset closed my file, thus concluding our interview.

"Well, some of our girls do take a while to adjust to college life after public high school." Her voice sounded weary, perhaps from years of wardendom. "I'm sure you can bring your grades up with a little more diligence. Don't be afraid to ask for help. That's what we're here for." Free of her office, I pulled on my coat and woolen gloves and banged open the heavy door of Main Hall into bitter air. She's right, I thought. I was never smart enough to be here. I pulled my scarf tighter and bit down hard on my lower lip. I wanted only to go home.

But I didn't go home. Haunted by fear of disgracing the family, not to mention Great Aunt Alice, by either leaving Vassar or flunking out, I worked constantly. I avoided English classes and would never have dared to brave the forbidding

30

Miss Lockwood who challenged students to think critically on their own. When the library closed in the evening, I often smuggled reserve books out under my coat, furtively slipping them back the next day before I was caught. Once I even tucked a paper crammed with organic chemistry formulas inside my glasses case for use during an exam. But when the hour began, horrified at the risk I was taking, I left the case unopened and never tried it again. Later, I settled on American Culture as a major, not so much for genuine interest in the subject, but because there was no final exam. Gradually my grades improved. And I made friends.

At first, the question of who belonged to what group was not always obvious; I had to learn how and where the lines were drawn. Being a year younger and from a West Coast public school, I learned that I didn't belong to the private school girl cliques who spoke a language of their own. They wore Bermuda shorts and argyle knee socks, and after dinner sat cross-legged on the parlor floor playing bridge and laughing at private jokes. On weekends away, they wore fur coats. Before I left home, Mother had unearthed a fur coat from a trunk in our dank-smelling store room, but when the fur began to come out in tufts, we gave it to Goodwill.

Soon I gravitated into a group of my own. There was my roommate, Diane, whose father was a three-star general. There was Maryanne, the girl down the hall, who had taken the train from Michigan. There was Sally, the daughter of a chicken farming family from upstate New York. And there was Becca, Sally's roommate. Becca would never have fitted into the 1952 *Vassar Bulletin*. Never had I been close to someone who dared to dress differently, who threw coffee mugs when she was angry, or who wasn't afraid to hang out with a philosophy teacher who looked like a novelist. And never had I known a friend who was Jewish, who laughed so easily or hugged so hard. Nonetheless, she swooped me up, took me under her wing, and invited me to her home where I was welcomed for holiday weekends.

So I was suprised when one Saturday after dinner, I knocked on her door. "What are you doing tonight? Want to go to a movie?" Becca was fastening long earrings in the mirror over her bureau, her hair coiled loosely. Her Bohemian skirt barely touched sandaled feet and her eyes were deep in olive tinted skin.

"Sorry, I can't." Becca examined her mouth. "I have a date tonight."

"Who with?"

"Remember that doctor guy, David, I see sometimes? He's up from New York."

I remembered once passing a dark-haired, handsome man waiting for Becca in the formal living room downstairs. I wondered if he smelled of after-shave lotion, what it would be like to kiss him. "Oh, lucky you," I sighed. "Maybe he has a friend for next time? We could double date."

Becca glanced at me. "I'm sorry. He doesn't have friends who'd want to go out with you." Stung by the rejection, I looked at her blankly. She fiddled with an earring. "You're not Jewish."

"So?"

"David and his friends are looking for wives. They don't want to spend time with someone who isn't Jewish. That's just the way it is."

I missed the casual dating I was used to at home, but I began to get the hang of Vassar's social life. By junior year, I was more at ease in a dating scene that took place at men's colleges where we traveled by bus or hired limousines to vanish into entire weekends of football or house parties fueled by alcohol. We yelled in stadiums for teams we cared nothing about, idolized the Yale Whiffenpoofs, drank scotch, and danced and necked late into the night, warmly damp and breathing hard. There were pitfalls. One mortifying weekend, I arrived at Harvard, dead tired and hungry after a week of classses. My date, a nice young man from home, took me immediately to a party in someone's room where they were serving a punch consisting of scoops of vanilla ice cream floating in something lethal, possibly straight gin. Vanilla ice cream has always been my undoing. I am chagrined to confess that I remember nothing after that party until Sunday morning when I was alert enough for the young man, who had spent the weekend alone, to bundle me onto a bus that delivered me back to school.

Spending an entire weekend with the same date, especially a blind date, could be a challenge. Women were supposed to be alluring and flirtatious, but sexually unavailable. Raised in a family where talk about bodily functions, especially sex, was unthinkable, and the process of menstruation was known as "the curse," my sources of information were scant. If a book like *Our Bodies Ourselves* had been available to consult when I was young, I would never have looked up the intriguing word "extremeties" in the dictionary, only to discover, to my disappointment, that it only meant "hands and feet." Birth control was hard to find or didn't exist; abortions were illegal and unsafe. Good girls like me stayed with a friend, a relative, or in boarding houses that supposedly had some kind of supervision, though I never saw any evidence of a chaperone. Terrified of getting pregnant, I had to learn where to draw the line, and managed to remain chastely innocent throughout.

In the middle of my junior year, seniors began to return from weekends sporting diamonds on their left hands, a phenomenon I considered with interest. I began to wonder with an edge of concern what I would do next year after graduation. Some classmates who weren't already engaged planned to go to graduate school; my roommates talked of looking for jobs in the crowded excitement of New York. Both ideas were overwhelming to me. How would I manage? What skills could I offer? Without thinking it out loud or even to myself, I knew in my heart that what I really wanted was the security of marrying and becoming a mom. I was ready to fall in love.

Finger Bowls and Caviar

"You should meet my older brother, Parks," said my friend Devon, a melancholy looking junior at Yale, whose finely chiseled profile could have come straight out of an F. Scott Fitzgerald novel. Devon lived in New Haven with my Aunt Bernice. Never my favorite aunt, she was a plain, gossipy woman with a fascination for the minutiae of life, but to her credit, she was kind and liked to take in Yale students who wanted to live away from the intensity of campus life. I often saw Devon when I took the bus from Vassar to visit Aunt Bernice during college breaks and had nowhere else to go. She told me he was in love with a rich girl from New York who wore a size 2, and that his family lived on the Upper East Side.

Devon told me his first girl friend had been NOCD. "It means Not Our Class Dear," he explained. He said it was a family joke, but it was hard to tell if he was being funny or not. And he talked about his brother. "His name is Parker D. Holt, Jr. after Dad, but everyone calls him Parks. He's smart, magna cum laude from Princeton. Good looking too. He's a graduate student here in English, started last fall. I could set you up for a date with him some time when you're down, if you'd like." Only just eighteen, I was impressed.

Devon was right. Parks was indeed handsome in the traditional Ivy League crew neck sweater kind of way. But he wasn't the frat "white shoe" type either; I was immediately drawn to a fleeting little-boy look behind his grey eyes. His brown hair was neatly trimmed, and when he put on horn-rimmed reading glasses and smoked a pipe, he looked very grown up, like a professor teaching a class. On our first date, one of those grim February afternoons when dirty snow piles against curbs and cars grind through slush, he took me to a Jimmy Stewart movie.

"Do you like Chinese food?" he asked when we came blinking out of the theater into a cheerless dusk. "We could get take-out and go up to my room and talk. Unless you want to get back to see Aunt Bernice." When he smiled at me, I knew he was joking, and in his room on the second floor of a boarding house, it felt natural to curl up on the Madras-covered daybed and eat chow mein and rice out of cartons. I pretended I knew how to use chopsticks while he talked about how wonderful his parents were, and about his senior thesis on Joseph Conrad's *Heart of Darkness*. I thought a book about a murky African river sounded depressing, but he was smart and I liked to watch him tap and refill his pipe. He could be funny too, and made me laugh when he imitated Jimmy Stewart's drawl. The lost look in his eyes was back when he told me how lonely he was without his Princeton roommates and how scared he was of failing Old English at Yale. That I could understand.

"I know exactly how you feel," I said, and told him about my English paper on "Chain Mail in Beowulf." When I reached to press his hand, he put his arm around me and we leaned into a tentative kiss. I can make Parks happy, I thought, with my eyes still closed. We're perfect for each other. A natural fit.

During the next two months, Parks drove twice to Vassar to see me, and by the time snow was melting and spring was pushing daffodils out of frozen earth, he invited me to have dinner with him and his parents at their apartment in New York. Afterwards, he told me, we would all drive to their "country house" for the weekend in New Jersey. His mother even sent me a monogrammed note of welcome. What could be better than that? I wondered. With their trips to the Bahamas and dinners at '21', the Holt family's air of expensive privilege was a magnet for me.

The apartment elevator man touched his hat as he slid back the gate and opened the metal grill. "Here you are, Miss." Parks had told me the man's name was Robert.

"Thank you," I murmured, wondering if I should call him Robert and deciding not. I felt a wave of panic. If I turned around now, I thought, I could ride down with him, take the subway to Grand Central and catch a train back to Vassar. Instead, I stepped resolutely into the warm fifth floor foyer outside the apartment door, while behind me, Robert closed the gate and rattled the elevator inexorably away. Furniture polish mingled with a faint odor of freshly baked cookies, and over a shining table holding a bowl of fresh tulips, an oval mirror reflected my face staring blankly back. I checked my teeth for lipstick, a vivid red meant to match my high heels and leather belt. It makes my face look pale, I thought, and pinched both cheeks hard. With a final pat to my hair, always too short for a stylish pageboy, and a deep breath for courage, I rang the bell. Almost immediately there stood a smiling maid, a little stooped, wearing the kind of uniform I had only seen in movies, black taffeta, with a white half apron and starched cap balanced on her graying frizzed hair.

"Ahhh, Gawd love us, look at ya now standing there, young as can be and fresh out of the subway are ya?" Her eyes twinkled at me behind her bifocals. "Come along in now, dear, and let me take yer coat." I struggled out of my khaki raincoat and watched her tuck it and my suitcase into the hall closet next to what I thought must be a mink fur. I was sucking in my stomach, round from too many starchy dormitory meals, when there was a sharply sophisticated voice around the corner of the living room. The maid had disappeared.

"Meredie? Is that you?" Mrs. Holt accompanied her voice, advancing into the hall with her hand outstretched. "You're right on time. I'm sorry Parks couldn't be here when you came. He's told us you're from California. Do come in."

Following Mrs. Holt into the living room, I tried to take in her straight-backed beauty, expensive blue-grey hair, her flowered silk blouse above tailored pants and soft suede evening slippers. My beige wool traveling dress that had seemed so stylish when Mother and I picked it out last summer felt frumpy. I sensed rather than smelled Mrs. Holt's delicate perfume, and fervently wished Parks were there too. "I'm going to be a little late," he had apologized, "but I can't miss that last class. Don't worry, though, you're going to absolutely love Mom and Dad." I desperately wanted them to love me back.

The cozy living room was a fishbowl of light. Matching pastel-hued furniture was grouped around a cheerful fireplace, and sheer curtained windows at the far end looked out on the city. A large secretary desk in one corner held silver framed family photographs. I would have liked to stare for hours at New York, its windows rectangles of gold suspended in the darkness, but Mr. Holt was getting up to meet me. Everything about him was made of angles, I thought, as we shook hands. His shrewd eyes behind their glasses and his beaked nose above the straight lines of his stockbroker's suit bore into me with an unfamiliar air of power.

"Well, Meredie, nice to meet you. That boy's always late. Class or no class, it's a bad habit. What'll you have to drink?" I looked at his glass on the coffee table next to a monogrammed ashtray and a silver cigarette box. "Canadian Club? Do you like it on the rocks?" he persisted. I'd never heard of Canadian Club, but stiff with tension, I nodded to be safe and took a chair facing him. In a moment, the maid was standing next to me with a plate of gooey black fish eggs balanced on some rounds of Melba Toast. I chose one gingerly and smiled up at her, relieved to see her again.

"Ahh, Gawd, dear, take two, ya must be famished."

"Best caviar in New York," said Mr. Holt, handing me my drink. "Do you like caviar? We'll be getting the best damn blue fish down in Red Bank this weekend, straight out of the sea. If you're having something, you've got to have the best, don't you think?" I struggled to think of an answer, but he changed the subject abruptly. "So you met Moonie? Her real name is Marian, but everyone calls her Moonie. Except Clare." He glanced at his wife. "Moonie's been with us since Parks was a baby. And when his brothers, the twins, came along, I don't know what we'd have done without her. She took care of them as if they were her own children, isn't that right, Pie?" This seemed to be a family of nicknames.

"That's right," said Mrs. Holt quietly from her chair across from me, and I wondered for a moment if she could be jealous of her maid for being a second mother to the boys. There was the sound of the front door opening, and with relief, I heard Parks's voice in the hall imitating the maid's accent followed by her peel of cackling laughter in reply.

"Ahh, Moonie, how are ya now, dear? Give me a hug and tell me how yer friend the Pope might be." Then he was in the doorway smiling at me. My heart jumped, but not wanting to seem eager, I stayed in my seat.

"Hello, Mummy. Hi, Dad. Sorry I'm late. You know what New Haven trains are like on a Friday night."

"Well, for Chrissake," said his father, "Hurry up if you want a drink. Moonie'll have dinner ready any minute."

Parks bent down to Mrs. Holt who offered her cheek for his kiss, and I watched him take a seat on the couch across from me. He smiled again and winked. He and his mother looked alike, I thought, but Parks's good looks were gentler, while his mother was regal, her blue eyes keen. I secretly admired her gold bracelet and earrings studded with green emeralds and diamonds, and when she lit a cigarette, I lit one too. I crossed my legs like hers, hoping the seams of my nylons were straight. I had never seen anyone so elegant in my life.

"Filthy habit, that smoking," Mr. Holt declared, more to his wife than to me. But Moonie was announcing dinner in a soft, formal voice.

"Thank you, Marian," said Mrs. Holt. The family seemed to treat Moonie with a mixture of jocularity and formality that was confusing. At dinner, I sat across from Parks, our faces almost hidden behind tall candlesticks, their polished silver mirrored in the table's surface. Mrs. Holt sat under her own life-sized portrait. Perfectly poised in a straight chair with '20's style flapper hair cropped close, her likeness stared down on us with an expression as smooth as the lush red velvet of her dress. I wondered what it was like to sit underneath yourself every day. While Moonie was clearing the table and passing around flowered dessert plates, each with a crystal glass bowl, Mr. Holt turned unexpectedly to me to inquire about my favorite opera. Caught off guard, I summoned the only opera I could think of. "Aida."

"Leontyne Price?"

I nodded, praying he wouldn't ask for the name of the tenor, but he was distracted. Moonie was standing next to me with a serving dish of dessert and a silence had fallen over the table. Everyone was looking at me. Finally, she leaned down to my ear. "Move yer bowl, dear, move yer bowl."

I glanced around. Everyone had moved their finger bowls to one side except me. Hot with frustration that I hadn't been paying attention, I hastily moved the offending bowl. Before I left home, Mother had carefully explained the old fashioned etiquette of finger bowls after the last course of a formal meal. There was another pause. Moonie leaned down again, but before she could say anything, I grabbed up the paper doily that had been left behind and moved that too. A sigh of expelled relief went around the table.

"Well, we got through that round," chided Mr. Holt.

"I know perfectly well how to use finger bowls," I started, trying to explain that I was sure mine hadn't had water in it. But no one was listening. I wondered what other rounds of mishaps Mr. Holt was talking about and whether or not I had gotten through them.

Finally dinner was over, and while Parks and his parents were collecting their things for the New Jersey weekend, I decided to go to the kitchen to say goodbye to Moonie. Slipping down a short hallway past her sparse bedroom with Jesus hanging on a cross over a steel frame bed, and through a swinging door, the kitchen was as immaculate as if a roast beef dinner had never been served. In one corner, a round gnome of a man was perched on a stool, his domed head shiny as a car's headlight, pink ears sticking out on either side. Shaking his hand, I looked at Moonie quizzically.

"Ah, you haven't met Pete, have ya? He comes up the service elevator behind the pantry some evenings for a visit. Now don't you go making eyes at Meredie, will you, Pete?" Moonie leaned her head back with laughter, and Pete, chuckling and blushing, shook his head. I laughed too, relieved to be relaxing into this friendly place. I hardly noticed Mrs. Holt looking into the kitchen, her eyes an ice blue, and that Moonie's hand was on my back, gently propelling me towards the swinging door. I didn't know you weren't supposed to say goodbye to a maid.

It wasn't until Moonie had retired many years later that I learned the truth about Pete. He was not Moonie's boyfriend as the Holt family had always assumed. Afraid she would be fired if they knew the truth, Moonie had concealed during the forty years she worked for them that she was secretly married to Pete and that together they had raised a son.

Betrothal

Troth Made Known
Vassar Senior will be Bride
of Parker Davenport Holt, Jr.,
Princeton Alumnus
—The *New York Times*, August 6, 1955

I have no memory of how we became engaged in the middle of that blissful summer following my junior year. Yearning for the safety of family, I had taken the twelve-hour flight home to Altadena when school was out, and Parks, having dropped out of Yale after he failed Old English, followed me to California to pursue our romance.

Perhaps I was the one who started a sentence one evening with, "After we're married," and he had agreed. Or perhaps he mentioned it first. However it happened, I became a nineteen-year old bride-to-be with the coveted diamond ring on my left hand. My parents announced our engagement to friends at an evening party by the pool, and I was thrilled when my photograph and our engagement notice appeared, just like a society bride, in the *New York Times*.

It was hard to know during those carefree weeks if Parks was more in love with my parents or with me. Mother and Dad were entranced by this Ivy League young man with all the right credentials, and wrapped him in the comforting cocoon of a summer at 596. Through soothing days of sun-drenched swims in the pool, gin and tonics under the patio arbor, and trips to the beach, Mother cooked casseroles and dispensed hugs while my gently attentive father sat with Parks for hours, absorbed in dissecting his life and the question of what he should do with it.

Years later, Mother would tell me about a single incident I knew nothing about that had occurred during those euphoric weeks. It seems that Parks had asked her to go with him to our

43

finest Pasadena department store where together they chose an engagement gift for me, a glamorous red velvet dress. But within a day, Parks was gripped with agonizing indecision. Perhaps he had made the wrong choice. Perhaps he should take it back. After hours of discussion and two abortive trips to the store, Mother finally persuaded him to keep the dress to give to me on the eve of our wedding. Unknown to me, she tucked away her private concerns about his mental stability, so that months later, I would dance, carefree and radiant, in my beautiful red velvet dress.

Summer was coming to an end, and decisions about Parks's immediate future loomed. His father was on the phone more than once urging him to enlist in the army. The Korean War had ended and the draft had dwindled, but Mr. Holt, perhaps believing the army would toughen Parks up, persuaded him that his plan made sense. "Take a break," he said. "You could get drafted now that you're not in school. Volunteer and get it over with before they draft you. Then go back to Yale."

In September, I flew back to Vassar, with little idea of who I was or what I was doing, except that I was secure in my diamond ring and had one year to go. I had classes to finish and exams to take. And there was a growing apprehension about my senior thesis, an intimidating prospect. I'd chosen to write on the Japanese-American Internment in World War II, but had no idea how to find the camp survivors my advisor urged me to interview when I was home that next Christmas vacation.

Meanwhile, Parks, a miserably unlikely soldier at best, reported for infantry training at New Jersey's Fort Dix. Physically soft from the summer, he stumbled through enforced marches, crawled under barbed wire, and learned how to use an M-1 rifle to kill. Throughout that fall, we lived for the few weekends he had off, and on Sunday nights clung to each other in a deserted Grand Central Station, my tearful cheek pressed against the unfamiliar roughness of his khaki uniform as he wept into my hair. His misery consumed us both. There was little time to think about the future or what it would be like to be a wife, an army wife at that. Maybe a wedding at 596 some time next summer, I thought vaguely, if I thought at all, while I wrote *Mrs. Parker D. Holt, Jr.* on the margins of class notes.

No one knew where Parks's advanced training division would be sent after boot camp until he called me one December evening sounding as if he were choking on a chicken bone. "My unit has its orders," he wept into the phone. "In two months we're being shipped to Korea." How, I wondered, could he survive such an ordeal? How could I? "We have to get married before I go," he was saying and through my tears, I heard myself agreeing. Together, with the dogged determination of a Romeo and Juliet about to be parted, and many phone calls later, we persuaded our families that we should be married during Vassar's Christmas vacation and Parks's four-day leave.

Suddenly, everyone I knew took part in a fast-forward film as if it were a matter of life or death. In the name of patriotism, the Warden, perhaps in deference to Great Aunt Alice, broke precedent by reluctantly giving me permission to be married while I finished my senior year. I forgot my plans to interview internment camp survivors at Christmas and spent most of my time on the phone. "You're missing out on the fun of your senior year," said one of my roommates unhelpfully, but I couldn't let myself believe this was true.

Unaccustomed to travel, my mother summoned the courage to take the train east for the first time since I'd been at Vassar, and incredibly managed to pull together a formal wedding to be held in New Haven where Aunt Bernice and my grandmother lived. It was not where I would have chosen, but by then I had no choice. A church was found. Invitations were sent. My four faithful roommates rose to the occasion to be bridesmaids. My sister Annie agreed to be maid of honor,

45

and my brother Thad joined Parks's Princeton roommates as an usher. Between classes, I squeezed in a bridal shower, lunches, formal newspaper photographs and two wedding dress fittings in New York. Driven by numb disbelief and the drama of it all, I was riding a high-speed train with no idea of where it was going or how to get off.

"Hold still, now, dearie," said the seamstress through a mouthful of pins.

"I think I'm going to faint," I murmured, crushing yards of lacey white as I sank onto a nearby stool with my head between my knees. Then there was the dreaded matter of birth control. Mortification knew no end when Mother consulted Aunt Bernice, who insisted that, time being short, she would make me an appointment with her own gynecologist. "Oh, please don't," I protested, but in the end I gave up, and blushing furiously, allowed an elderly gentleman wearing a pince-nez to measure me for a diaphragm on a steel table while I stared at the ceiling and wished myself onto a distant island. Some place with palm trees and lots of sun.

The last harried week included a ladies' luncheon at the Fifth Avenue mansion of Parks's grandmother, a formidable woman whose matriarchal jowls could have been mistaken for an Engish bulldog's. Mother, dressed in an almost sophisticated navy blue suit and high heels that must have killed her feet, outdid herself in the grandmother's drapery-shrouded dining room where eighteenth century portraits, perhaps of male Holts, stared down from the walls, and maids came and went. Mother glided gracefully through three courses that included a finger bowl, and talked with my future mother-in-law as if they'd known each other all their lives. "Mom, you were wonderful!" I said, once we were safely outside. She turned to me with a twinkle as she lit a cigarette.

"Don't ever forget. Our blood is just as blue as their blue blood."

Three days before Christmas, a blizzard left the New Haven landscape sparkling beneath a blanket of snow. Somehow a respectable number of guests were able to make their way to the church at the appointed hour, many of whom I had never seen in my life. At the door of the church, I waited on my father's arm as if anesthetized for the wedding march to begin, and with the first chords, the bridesmaids balanced gracefully towards the altar on their matching linen high heels. In front of me, Annie stood stiff-backed in pale blue with an uncharacteristic flower in her hair. Old guilt was uncovered at this last moment and I wanted to hug her, to tell her I loved her, that I shouldn't be the one marrying first. There was no time. "Annie," I whispered instead, "I'm so proud of you." I never seemed to say what I meant to say, and she sent me one startled glance before starting down the aisle. Dad's arm felt damp under his suit when it was our turn, and before I knew it, I was standing at the altar next to an adoring Parks whose face was only a blur. We said our vows, I guess there was a prayer, and I became Mrs. Parker Davenport Holt, Jr.

But Parks never went to Korea. The good-old-boy-network, where powerful men in powerful places do favors for other powerful men, had swung into high gear. It seems that Parks's father was friends with Richard Helms, a tough-jawed senior official in the Central Intelligence Agency, and that the following took place:

- Mr. Holt invited Mr. Helms to lunch in New York.
- Mr. Helms invited a general in the Pentagon to drinks in Washington.
- The general in the Pentagon called the colonel in command of Fort Dix.
- The colonel wrote orders to the major in charge of Parks's unit.

– Parks was transferred from Fort Dix to Washington D.C. where he finished out the remainder of his military service in a coat and tie.

Twenty years later, Mr. Helms would hold the dubious distinction of being the only director of the CIA convicted of lying to Congress.

Parks and I celebrated this amazing good fortune with a bottle of champagne, but I had to let go of a secret fantasy that while Parks was in Korea, I could live snugly at home with my parents and write heroic daily letters to my husband overseas. Instead, after graduating from Vassar, Parks and I moved into a small apartment outside of Washington and I took a job answering phones at the Stanford Research Institute's East Coast office. Parks did whatever CIA people do behind a government desk.

One painful weekend, my father-in-law persuaded us to invite Mr. Helms and his wife to our apartment for dinner as a thank you for Mr. Helms's largesse. The phone rang that afternoon while I fished bay leaves and whole garlic cloves out of my first attempt at a beef bourguignon, and a deep voice inquired if they should dress for dinner. "Oh, no, Mr. Helms, please, no, of course not," I stuttered in a flood of horror at the idea of their arriving at our walk-up apartment wearing formal evening clothes. It was bad enough they were coming at all.

"This is *Mrs.* Helms," said the voice, husky from cigarettes.

Ivy League of the West

We had been locked in one of our draining indecisions about the future. Now that he was close to finishing his army stint with the CIA, it was taken for granted that Parks would go back for a Ph.D. and become a professor on an Ivy League campus. His father was determined that he go back to study at Yale, Mr. Holt's own alma mater. "I don't know what happened that year you failed Old English," he said. "But you know Yale's the best in the country. Let's see you get back on the horse and show them your stuff." The last place I wanted to live was New Haven within visiting distance of Aunt Bernice.

"Let's move to California," I begged. "Maybe you could even teach in a high school." Our eyes held each other.

"Well, I don't know," said Parks, shifting in his chair and looking away. "There are lots of reasons I should go back to Yale." I sighed. Any dream I might have nursed about his teaching in some prep school where I could be a cozy dorm mom surrounded by students telling me their troubles, had evaporated. I knew I'd have an ally in my mother, and, sure enough, when I telephoned her, she rose to the challenge like a trout to a fly. She repeatedly urged Parks to apply to Stanford where, on the opposite coast from his parents, she was convinced he would be free of his chronic anxiety. Finally, after much back and forth, while sandstone arches and sun-dappled palm trees beckoned, Parks submitted an application and was accepted to the graduate program in English at Stanford.

"My God," said Mr. Holt, joking to cover his disappointment. "How are you going to get your mail? By Pony Express?"

"Very funny," we said, and in the fall of 1957, with me, at the age of twenty-two, queasy from morning sickness, and

Parks taut with apprehension, we moved to the West Coast. We had broken a mold.

But graduate school in California was not the convivial, joyful life I had imagined. We rented a stucco house on a treeless street in Menlo Park that turned out to be a boring box of a place, more appropriate for a retired couple and their cat than for a pregnant young couple looking for community. Parks' brother, Devon, would have said it was NOCD. Other students tended to live in graduate housing and form their own groups. No matter how hard I tried, I could never make our living room feel cozy with our cheap Salvation Army couch that mixed oddly with two Danish armchairs, wedding gifts from the Holts. In the backyard, an uninviting crab grass yard contained a garage, a metal clothesline and a dispirited looking apple tree.

Far from feeling liberated, Parks worked constantly. His need to prove himself to his father, either real or imagined, hung over him at every turn. For my part, I agreed to a temporary clerical job at the Stanford Research Institute home office that would come to an end when the baby was born. It was at the height of the Cold War, and I was assigned to a back office where I filled in columns with projected numbers of people doomed to annihilation by nuclear bombs of varying kilotons. Alone in the office, while my unborn infant kicked inside me, I stared at the figures with no comprehension of what they meant. A sense of numbing unreality settled over me during those months that would recur throughout our marriage. Not a good start to our new life in the Golden State.

We hadn't been at Stanford long before there was an invitation from the Wallace Stegners to lunch at their home in the Los Altos Hills. Famous for his novels and short stories, Mr. Stegner was a professor of creative writing at Stanford on a pinnacle so high, I could barely see his feet. The Stegners were friends of a branch of my father's East Coast cousins who summered together every year at a lake in picturesque Greensboro, Vermont. I imagined Mr. Stegner writing his novels in a comfortably rustic cabin by day, and by evening, joining his wife and other professorial families for cocktails on someone's deck or perhaps a moonlit canoe paddle to the strains of classical music broadcast across the lake. It was a duty invitation to Parks and me that I recognized as proper behavior for well-brought up people.

We arrived at the stroke of noon. "What a beautiful house," we exclaimed at least three times in admiration of the Stegners' paneled living room and spacious deck built around an oak tree and overlooking the valley. Cumbersome in a new maternity smock, I studied the way our hosts exuded a casual non-elegance in their soft-hide loafers and woven tweeds. *Sunset Magazine* had come to life just like the one on their glass coffee table, and I resisted the urge to kick off my high-heeled shoes and curl barefoot into one of the cushioned chairs.

Mrs. Stegner served lunch on Mexican pottery as effortlessly as if she had waved a magic wand. The quiche was a perfect shade of brown, the cucumber salad delicious, and for dessert, a sherbet I'm sure was homemade. If I just work hard enough, I thought, I can make a home like this. I still remember Professor Stegner, relaxed in a cardigan sweater with leather elbow patches, puffing on his pipe and observing us with the genial amusement of a golden retriever looking after a couple of pups. When it was over, we thanked them effusively, and never saw them again.

Twenty years later, Professor Stegner would publish *Crossing to Safety*, his brilliant autobiographical novel based on his friendship with my father's Greensboro cousins.

Our best friends at Stanford were Rowland and Sam, an unlikely pair of Mutt-and-Jeff type fellow graduate students. Rowland was affectionately relaxed with thinning hair and a broad waist that made him look middle-aged before his time, and Sam, shyly gawky with his flattop haircut and big ears, just wanted to be wherever Rowland was. That they might be gay never entered my head. I did know that I looked forward to their visits to our house while Sam shifted from foot to foot and grinned and Rowland and I gossiped together, shared recipes and family news. He had greeted our baby boy's arrival as if he had been his own.

Baby Mac wasn't born in the car, but it was close. As eagerly as I had longed for this little one, I was curiously unprepared. I had left no doctor's number to call, no written directions to the hospital waiting on the kitchen sink. There were only blinking stoplights across deserted streets, Parks's repeated, "Where is this goddamn place," excruciating pain, squealing tires, and someone calling for a wheelchair. Then, a long hallway, "You can't go in there," to Parks, and a nurse scolding me, "Stop making so much noise," before I was put out.

Parks's grandmother was outraged when we named our baby, Malcolm Parker Holt. "How could you ignore our family lineage by not naming him Parker Davenport Holt, III, like other young parents?" And besides, "Why did you name him Malcolm? Our family isn't even Scotch!" Unless we changed his name, we were told, she would not be sending her new great-grandson the traditional baby cereal bowl, a silver porringer. Eventually, who knows why, she did relent and a Tiffany turquoise box arrived in the mail. But the porringer had not been engraved with the baby's initials. Instead, a small card was enclosed: To the little boy with the dreadful name.

But memory is a curious phenomenon. I have only the dimmest recollection of the hard parts of early motherhood. Never, to my mind, was there anything or anybody as remarkable as this baby we had produced. It didn't occur to me that I could barely take care of myself much less a tiny human completely dependent on me for his every need. My own mother wasn't there to help, my father having fallen ill with the flu at home. My mother-in-law was not an option since she had stated from the outset that she didn't like babies until they had turned at least two. There was no encouragement from the hospital staff when they brought my newborn to nurse, no comforting support groups when I came home. But it didn't matter. I believed myself to be a naturally talented mother and that I could do this all by myself. I have almost forgotten the exhaustion of getting up at night, or that I didn't have enough breast milk and had to make formula. I had to boil glass bottles, twelve at a time, on the back of the stove. The loneliness of walking Mac in his black plaid baby buggy up and down Menlo Park's deserted Arbor Road is only a vague mist in the back of my mind.

I do remember the satisfaction of bathing him in the kitchen sink, of wrapping his small body in a flannel "receiving blanket" like a Christmas gift, and carrying him on my hip in the "football hold" I had been taught in baby class. And I loved it when Parks and I snuggled him before bed. Still pinkish from his bath, Mac regarded us placidly with eyes that were turning as brown as mine and rewarded us with deep chortles when Parks blew spluttering noises onto his tummy. I could have stayed there forever, the three of us curled around each other in the middle of our bed.

The Chairman Comes to Dinner

It might have been our lunch at the Wallace Stegners that inspired Parks. "I've got an idea," he said one evening while we ate a spaghetti supper and three-month-old Mac squirmed on my lap. "I think we should invite Sherman Wetherby for dinner." I stared at Parks in disbelief.

"Professor Wetherby? The Department Chairman? Here?"

"It's a nice gesture," Parks said. "It'll be easy. We'll invite Sam and Rowland, and you can make a leg of lamb. Or something like that." I stared out the window at the laundered diapers hanging over the crabgrass.

"Well, I don't know," I started, but in my heart I did know. If a husband wants to have his boss for dinner, it's up to the wife to prepare a dinner for the boss. Maybe if Rowland and Sam were there, it would be all right. Their reassuring presence always made me feel more like family. For a week, in between cooing and changing, I poured anxiously over *The Joy of Cooking*, a hand-me-down from my mother. Finally, ignoring the cost, I decided on a braised leg of lamb with onions and carrots, scalloped potatoes, peas, hot rolls, green salad and a pecan pie. An alarming prospect. I'd have to buy the pie. Never having done anything with a potato except bake it, I made Parks eat two rehearsals of the scalloped potatoes before I was satisfied.

When the bell rang Saturday night at 7:00 sharp, Sam, his hands in his back pockets, loomed tall and self-conscious in a new sweater. Next to him, Rowland, wearing a coat and tie for the occasion, enveloped me in a comforting hug. Back in the bedroom, rocking and humming to Mac, I tightened with nervousness when the doorbell rang again. "I have to go," I whispered to my sleeping baby, and slipped reluctantly from the bedroom to find Parks helping the professor out of his coat.

"How d'you do, how d'you do?" Professor Wetherby shook my hand damply.

"I'm glad to meet you," I said without conviction, looking down into pale slits of eyes behind rimless glasses. The man was as short as he was prodigiously plump. Everything about him was round. Parks steered him into our small living room where he perched on the edge of the couch. Rowland leaned to straighten Sam's collar before he settled into one of the Danish arm chairs, while Sam took the other, crouching forward with hands on his knees as if he were ready to leap up at a moment's notice.

"A glass of wine, Professor Wetherby?" asked Parks. "Or would you prefer something stronger?" I passed around a plate of smoked oysters carefully arranged with a sprig of parsley.

"Oh, no, I couldn't possibly, not possibly," the professor stammered. "Strict diet. I'm on a very strict diet." He had a curious way of saying everything twice. "Nothing to drink, please, nothing to drink." He held up one dimpled hand to Parks. "Well, perhaps some soda water. Might you have some soda water?"

"I'll have a whiskey on the rocks," said Rowland firmly.

"Me too." said Sam.

Retreating to the kitchen, I took nervous swallows of wine as I pulled the salad from the fridge, heated the potatoes and spooned mint jelly into a dish. Sticky pots went on the back stoop. Mrs. Stegner never put a sticky pot on a backyard stoop in her life. During their second round of drinks, I poured myself another glass of wine and set the dishes on the table, the roast in front of Parks's place and other dishes squeezed in next to mine. "Dinner is served," I announced self-consciously, and while everyone took their places, I realized too late that the sun was dappling a row of diapers behind them on the line. Parks carved the first slice of lamb, and I let out a breath of relief when I saw the requisite faint pink blushing from the center. Mom would have been proud. But I had forgotten the butter on the kitchen counter and had to inch my way behind Professor Wetherby, only to find when I sat down that I had forgotten the mint jelly and had to squeeze past him once again.

He was telling Parks, "Just a small piece of meat please, very small. I'm on a diet, you know." The potatoes made the rounds, but Professor Wetherby, his nose twitching like a beagle's, shook his head before passing the dish to Sam. When Parks poured the wine, the professor covered his glass with his hand while Rowland and Sam dug into large helpings of everything.

Rowland turned to him. "I was impressed by the guest lecturer at the Shakespeare meeting the other evening, Professor Wetherby. Very enlightening, didn't you think?"

"Yes, yes, a distinguished gentleman. Most informative..." But the professor was clearly distracted. His eyes darted from plate to plate and his mouth moved in unison with Rowland and Sam's as they chewed. Nothing more was forthcoming until he held out his glass to Parks. "I will have some of that wine after all, I think." He watched appreciatively while his glass was filled, took a deep swallow and looked down at his plate. There was a pause while we all looked at his plate, and I wondered if I should offer to boil up the package of broccoli in the freezer. While I tried to think of something to say, I resisted the temptation to get up and check on the sleeping baby. They would probably never notice I was gone.

"I see Maynard Mack has a new article on Alexander Pope," said Parks finally, but the Chairman was fixated on the half eaten roast.

"I wonder if I might have some more of that delicious lamb. It's very good, really." Spooning out some mint jelly, he glanced around the table and pointed at the dish of scalloped potatoes next to Sam. "And perhaps some of those." Forehead creased with persperation, he pushed up his glasses as he leaned forward with devoted concentration. "I really shouldn't," I heard him murmur as he reached across the table for one more roll and a square of butter.

I waited until he had accompanied his final bite with a long swallow of wine before I stood to clear the table and bring in the pie. Everyone wanted coffee, Parks served generous portions of pie with vanilla ice cream, and I helped myself to another scoop of ice cream, comforted by the chilled sweetness melting down my throat. Professor Wetherby let out a contented sigh and Parks pushed back his chair. "Let's bring our coffee cups into the living room so we can relax in more comfortable chairs," he said.

"Lovely dinner, my dear. You must give me the recipe for those potatoes," said Professor Wetherby, patting my shoulder as he headed for the living room. I was blowing out the candles, when behind me there was a crashing noise followed by a muffled grunt and a moment of pure silence. In the living room, I found Parks, Rowland and Sam staring down at Professor Wetherby, who had plunged through the Danish chair's elastic supports onto the floor. His feet hung over the edge of the chair's frame, and his hands flapped helplessly on either side of the wooden arms.

"I can't get out, I can't get out." His voice was high pitched in its fervor. "I can't get out." A wail from the bedroom galvanized us into motion. With Parks holding down one side of the chair and me holding the other, Rowland and Sam braced their feet and pulled the professor into a vertical position as if he were emerging from a deep pond. Rowland clucked and fussed around him, straightening his glasses and patting his rumpled jacket into place while Parks began an explanation about how the chairs weren't very well made. I went to retrieve Mac who hung over my shoulder in a pink rage, snot dripping from his nose and his eyes screwed tight against the sudden light. Parks gestured at the couch, suggesting the professor might be more comfortable over there.

"I don't think so, no, it must be getting late."

"Oh, please don't go Professor Wetherby," I said, handing the baby to Parks. "I'm so sorry. Let's all sit down and have some more coffee." But Professor Wetherby was heading for the door, and I had no choice but to find his coat and drape it over his arm. The baby hiccupped into Parks' shirt.

"A lovely dinner, my dear, goodbye, I must be going," said the Chairman as he eased his way out the door, down the steps and disappeared into the gathering night.

Bitsy

Not long after the dinner for Professor Wetherby, we moved to an idyllic cottage Parks found advertised in the Stanford housing office. Made of adobe bricks, with tiled floors and a fireplace, it hid by itself near the end of a Los Altos country road that smelled of honeysuckle and reminded me of Altadena when I was young.

Afternoons when Parks was late, I carried Mac across a ditch of golden foxtail grass to the other side of the road. Leaning against a wooden fence, we watched fingers of ocean fog curl like waves into the crevices of the Peninsula's shadowing hills, while Mac waved his chubby fist at the evening commuter train whistling its way across open fields. Absorbed in my baby, I didn't mind being alone. But sometimes, back at the house, while Mac had his supper, I played Harry Belafonte on the victrola and danced to his haunting rhythms. "Day-o, day-ay-ay-o, Daylight come and me wan' go home." The music gave me a catch of longing in my throat that I quickly swallowed away. I never thought to suggest to Parks that we go out dancing together, and he never asked.

Our lives had settled into a kind of comfortable routine when one morning I realized that for the second month in a row, I had missed my period. Not that I was worried, I told myself, I hadn't been regular since Mac was born, but just to be sure, I checked in with my doctor. The next day, balancing seven month old Mac against my hip with one hand, the phone in the other, I called his nurse for the test results. "Let's see. Mrs. Holt. Yes, here it is. The results of your pregnancy test are positive. Congratulations!" Her voice sounded very far away.

"Are you certain?" I stammered. Mac reached to stuff the phone cord into his mouth. How could this be? Then I remembered how it could be. In a hurry a couple of months before, I had made a careless mistake with the hated diaphragm. "It won't matter," I had reassured myself. I never confessed it to Parks, and after a while I forgot about it. Now here I was pregnant. Again.

Eight months into this easy second pregnancy, I politely listened to my doctor's advice to stay quietly at home for the last month. But the next week I was on a plane. My New Haven grandmother was in Altadena on her annual visit to my parents, and I was determined to fly to Southern California to show off my beautiful boy to his great grandmother. "Everything will be fine," I said to Parks, ignoring the possibility that everything might not be fine at all. Indeed, coming back on Sunday, the turbulence on our flight was so severe that I heard myself praying out loud to a God I didn't know I knew. I held Mac tight against my heart to keep him from being airborne, while I kept my free hand pressed to my womb.

"Worse flight we ever had," reported the stewardess cheerfully, as badly shaken, we waited to deplane.

I don't remember what time that same night the contractions began. I do remember that Parks called Rowland before it was light, and he arrived, avuncular as ever, to look after Mac. A few hours later, Elizabeth Clare was born three weeks premature and two years earlier than planned. We brought her home and stood gazing into the bassinette at this diminutive being who weighed less than five pounds and snuffled into her blanket like a small pink rabbit. "That's too big a name for such a tiny baby," I said, unable to believe she was real. "She's just an itsy bitsy." And "Bitsy" she became.

Again, I believed I was the great Earth Mother who could take care of these babies myself. But it wasn't long before I was groping my way through a dense fog of exhaustion. Bitsy woke constantly throughout the night with that persistent newborn whimper that rapidly dissolves into a full-blown squall. At fifteen months old, Mac decided to give up his afternoon nap. Parks moved a cot out to the back patio so he could get enough sleep for his work. The more I worried, the less milk I had and the more Bitsy cried. And the more I cried too. More than Bitsy. If I can't take care of two babies by myself, I wondered, what can I do?

To my relief, it was my mother who came to the rescue. Sweeping Mac into her arms with hugs and songs, she persuaded me to give up my attempts at nursing and to buy ready-made formula. I hired a sitter to play with Mac in the mornings, and Parks moved back in. By the time Mother went home, Bitsy was happily drinking from bottles to make up for lost time, and blossoming into a sunny, cherubic infant with a smile for anyone who came her way. Proud of our perfect little family, I glued what seemed like a cute decal of Stanford "Indians" to the back window of our station wagon—a papa chief, a mama chief, and their two little "chiefs," all with happy, laughing faces, feathers and braids.

Berkeley Beginnings

When Parks was offered a position as an instructor at the prestigious University of California before he had completed his Ph.D., we were lured by views of the Bay through sweet smelling eucalyptus. But at frst, everything about Berkeley felt strange and new. In Stanford's bucolic Palo Alto, where wide, tree-lined streets looked more or less the same, the peaceful atmosphere felt suspended in time. By contrast, Berkeley, with its air of vitality and unrest, thrived on variety. In the hills, picturesque houses crowded together on narrow streets. Next to the university, mansion-size homes boasted lush gardens, and in the flatlands, working class and black neighborhoods stretched across the city to the edge of the Bay.

An invitation arrived two weeks after we had settled into a small rental squeezed behind another house in the Berkeley hills:

Your presence is requested for cocktails
at the home of
Professor and Mrs. Mark Salzman
at 5 pm on Sundays,
September 10, 17 and 24, 1960

"Do you think this means all three Sundays?" I asked, bewildered by the invitation.

"I think it's all of them," said Parks. "Salzman's the Chairman. This doesn't look like an invitation. It looks like a command for new faculty to meet the department. We'll need a babysitter three Sundays in a row."

Overwhelmed by trepidation, I suffered before each Sunday's party over what clothes to wear, and spent hours mixing and matching tightly belted skirts and tops so they would look different each time. New dress shoes turned out to be too small, but I wore them anyway. The only babysitter I could find was our landlady's gum-snapping teenager, whose very presence sent two-year-old Mac wilting with shyness under his bed. "It's 50 cents an hour," she said, looking around for the television we didn't have.

In the Salzmans' crowded living room high on the edge of a hill, Mrs. Salzman wandered about looking vaguely ethereal in filmy pastel, while I watched new faculty act as if they already knew everyone there. Helping themselves liberally to Professor Salzman's trays of cocktails, they seemed so confident that it was hard to tell who was new and who were the faculty we were supposed to meet. Feeling no less shy than Mac, but with my smile firmly in place, I shifted from foot to foot next to Parks, drinking too much wine and worrying about Mac, who sobbed harder each time we left. Parks looked eager, standing the way he always did with his head pitched earnestly forward, and I felt absurdly young. By the third Sunday, I had switched to gin.

We had been at the university less than a year when we fell in love with a shingled house tucked along a curving road that had just gone on the market. We didn't care that the narrow house with its small rooms, cramped kitchen and lack of storage was inadequate for a growing family. It had a view. It had an A-frame roof, an open loft over the living room, and a cozy stone fireplace. Looking at it from the grassy hillside across the street where the children could play, it could have been featured on a cover of *Sunset Magazine*. With a down payment financed by the Holts, we moved in.

At the university, Parks felt overwhelmed by the prospect of having to finish his doctoral dissertation while teaching a full load of classes. To avoid the pressure in the department where wisps of gossip floated along office corridors about who had tenure and who didn't, he worked at home in the small study we added behind the living room loft. He didn't say so exactly, but I knew he felt safer having me around. The sound of his feet going up and down the narrow stairs became a background rhythm to our family's life.

"Please, God, let it start." I fussed around the living room nervously straightening pillows and keeping an ear on Parks's study door for the sound of his typewriter. His dissertation was due at Stanford in three weeks and his typewriter had been silent too long. He had chosen to write what he called a definitive edition of a little known eighteenth century novel entitled *A Sentimental Journey Through France and Italy* by a consumptive-looking clergyman named Laurence Sterne, author of *Tristram Shandy*. I thought it a peevishly odd little book to merit so much attention for a Ph.D., but never said as much. Finally, it was finished, four hundred pages with exhaustive explanatory footnotes covering half of every page.

"I have to find a typing service," Parks worried, thumbing through the Yellow Pages.

"I could type it for you," I offered a little hesitantly, eyeing the thick manuscript. This was something I could do to help. My junior high typing teacher had said "Rhythm is everything," and I was proud of the keyboard speed I had mastered to the beat of *The Stars and Stripes Forever* in our eighth grade classroom. So it happened that after the kids had been put to bed, I spent evenings hunched over my Smith Corona at the dining room table methodically banging out Parks's edition of Laurence Sterne. Correcting mistakes meant erasing the original, then scraping each of five carbon copies with a razor blade before typing it again. If I didn't leave enough room for the footnotes, I had to redo the page. It seemed like a miracle when at last we finished, Parks passed his orals and was congratulated by everyone we knew. I was satisfied with the work. We had been a team.

After our early initiation into departmental social life in the Salzman's living room, we soon learned that another fundamental part of the tenure process was a constant round of faculty dinner parties that we were required to either go to or give. These took place on Saturday evenings where assistant professors without tenure hoped to impress full professors with tenure, and wives worked tirelessly to produce elegant sit-down dinners for eight. I spent hours spattering Julia Child's *Mastering the Art of French Cooking* with buttery grease while getting the best of such recipes as ratatouille, coq au vin, and cherries jubilee—complete with flaming brandy. The idea of throwing together a potluck and bringing along the kids simply did not exist. Everyone drank. A lot.

One early morning after a particularly alcoholic dinner party, I stood in our small kitchen pouring apple juice into sippy cups. Fuzzily contemplating stacks of sticky dishes with their remains of jubilee, I had a moment of truth. My family had always had hired help. Why didn't I? The next week I hired Gussie.

A Cleaning Lady

Every two weeks, she waited for me to pick her up. Gussie was one of a small group of cleaning ladies who rode the Number 7 bus up Euclid Avenue in the mornings, disappeared into shingled homes with views of the Bay, and in the afternoons, rode the bus back to the flats. There was no bench on the corner, so she stood patiently in her black-laced shoes if I happened to be a little late. With grey hair flattened into a bun at the base of her neck, she looked old enough to be my grandmother. A cloth coat, smoothed for years by her worn brown hands, covered her spare frame.

At the house, Gussie folded the coat and her handbag into a corner of the playroom bed, tied on her apron, fixed herself a cup of black coffee and went silently to work. I was reminded of May who worked for Mother, and of Proctor, digging around the trees, quietly unto himself. Tirelessly thorough, I never saw Gussie sit down, and after she left, a lingering smell of Pine-Sol made us feel safe and cared for. I always called her Gussie and she always called me Mrs. Holt. I knew she had a husband because once she said she might be late, "what with Mr. Preston having the gout." Maybe she has grandchildren, I thought, but I never knew how much to ask. Whenever Bitsy danced in from kindergarten, Gussie always beamed.

"Hiya there, Bizzy, don't you slip down now."

"Hi, Gussie, I won't." Bitsy didn't want to tell Gussie that Bizzy wasn't her name.

Our third baby, Rosemary, was born after Gussie had become a regular part of our life. An early snapshot of Rosie reveals a round-cheeked, pink and white baby, as blonde and blue-eyed as her brother and sister were dark. She observed the family she found around her with a quiet interest, knew what she wanted, and when things didn't go her way, let everybody know. She was devoted to her blanket and learned early to comfort herself by rubbing the binding against her cheek. Looking at Rosie staring back at her from her infant seat, Gussie would say, "I sure do love that child." One Christmas, I gave her a photograph of Rosie holding a daisy, and she said she'd "be proud" to keep it on her dresser where she could look at it every day.

Rosie was only a few months old when President Kennedy was killed. November 22, 1963. All that long, terrible weekend, Parks and I sat in front of the twelve inch TV in the playroom and mourned our president with the rest of the world. Again and again, we watched never-to-be-forgotten clips of Jackie in her pristine suit and pillbox hat reach across to her husband. Again and again, we heard Walter Cronkite choke out the paralyzing words, "President Kennedy died at one p.m. Central Standard Time." The images in black and white were stark.

Gussie came to clean that Monday, the day of Kennedy's funeral. "Oh, Gussie," I said as she lowered herself into the car. "I am so sorry." I said it twice, as if, in some way, this president belonged more to her than to me.

"Yes, ma'am." Her face was turned. In the silence, I wanted to pat her hand to show her we were in this together, but I was afraid my familiarity might intrude. Without taking off her coat, she went straight downstairs to the bedrooms below.

"Don't you want some coffee, Gussie?" I called, but there was no answer. Maybe she didn't hear, I thought. In the playroom, Parks, his face bleak, was on the bed with an arm around Mac and Bitsy and baby Rosie asleep on his knees. Together we watched the riderless horse and the caisson inch down Pennsylvania Avenue. Jackie followed between Bobby and Teddy, staring regally ahead through her black veil. They were like our own family, all first names to us.

"Why are the boots on that black horse pointing backwards?" Mac wanted to know. I put my finger to my lips. "I'll tell you later." The TV panned across the crowds and I studied each face, how each one carried its own sorrow, tears streaming or simply mute. What would it be like to have my private emotions displayed in front of the world? Two older black women leaned against each other, their hands pressed to their mouths, stoic in their grief.

My own hand went to my mouth. Gussie. She should be here with us.

"Mommy, where are you going?"

"I'll be right back." Downstairs, I found her scrubbing at the bathroom sink, her brush punishing the same faucet as if she'd never get it clean. "Gussie, please, won't you come up and watch the funeral with us and the children?" She turned briefly, her face expressionless behind traces of tears.

"No, Ma'am, I'm good here. When I hurt, I work."

"Are you sure? You should be with us."

"Yes, Ma'am. I'm sure."

"At least, won't you have something to eat? Some coffee?"

"No, Ma'am. I can't eat."

Back in the playroom, bagpipes wailed, the caisson rolled and I thought about the woman cleaning alone downstairs. Maybe I should ask her again. I tried to imagine her sitting on the bed next to us. Or would she let us bring her a chair? Or would she stand? I watched the Kennedy family, the somber dignitaries, the crowds of silent people, and felt layers of discomfort through my grief.

Every other Monday for the next year, Gussie came to clean. One afternoon, while Bitsy and Mac were still in school and Rosie was asleep, the phone rang. It was a woman with a voice like Gussie's. "Yes, this is Mrs. Holt," I replied. "Yes, Mrs. Preston works for me." Saying out loud that someone worked for me made me feel self-conscious.

"This is Mrs. Preston's daughter," said the woman. "I have to tell you…Something has happened." I listened, trying to understand. A stroke? Last Tuesday? The woman told me that getting off a bus near her house, Gussie's legs had given out and she had fallen down the steps onto the sidewalk. My free hand reached for the back of the chair.

"No," I said, and then, "No" again. Not Gussie. I thought about her cups of black coffee and her long hours of work. I should have made her rest.

The daughter stopped to take a breath. "She passed away right there on the sidewalk." I took a long breath too, the phone gripped tight. Gussie couldn't have died. On the sidewalk. By herself.

"The funeral is next Thursday. The sixteenth. My mother would have wanted you to come." I searched around for a pencil on my crowded desk. A church in Oakland. I wrote down the address. 2:00 o'clock. Parks would be teaching. I'd have to get a sitter.

"Thank you, of course I'll be there. I am so, so sorry." Say something more, I scolded myself. Maybe I did because the daughter thanked me more than once. When we hung up, I realized I had forgotten to ask her name.

The day of the funeral, the church was bigger than I expected. Coming in from the intense light of the sidewalk, I tried to adjust my eyes to what looked like an acre of pews that were just beginning to fill. I wasn't used to going places without Parks. Dark-skinned women in lacey or low-cut taffeta with shiny high heels and full-brimmed hats milled around the vestibule, hugging each other before pulling solemn children into pews. The air smelled of different kinds of cologne. Men greeted each other quietly, calling each other "Brother" with a grip to the shoulder and a shake of the hand. Everyone seemed to know everybody else.

A straight-backed man handed me a program and a fan with the name of the church inscribed on one side and Gussie's name and dates on the other. At the end of the center aisle, I was dismayed to see a white satin coffin with an open lid. I'd never seen an open coffin. How could Gussie be lying there? Would I have to go look at her? What do people do at a funeral in a black church? Feeling whiter than white in my navy blue sleeveless linen dress with its prissy Peter Pan collar and low-heeled pumps that could have been my mother-in-law's, I looked for somewhere to hide. I chose the back pew, lined with buttoned red cushions, and was pretending to study a hymnal when a full-bosomed woman under a purple hat in front of me swiveled around on one hip.

"Honey? Don't you sit back there all by yourself. You come sit up here now with us." From under the curve of her breast, a child's eyes fixed on me until his mother took hold of his head in one firm hand and turned him back.

"Oh, thank you, no, I'm fine, I mean…" Wooden timidity tied my tongue. "I may have to leave early," I lied, reaching to touch her shoulder in apology. But everyone was standing up as an organ boomed and a red-robed choir filed onto the stage. A minister in flowing robes took his place behind Gussie's coffin. I don't belong here, I thought. I could slip out now before the service starts. But then I remembered Gussie's daughter on the phone, "My mother would have wanted you to come." I stayed.

The preacher was thanking God for His blessings and for the Brothers and Sisters gathered there, all the while interrupted by murmurs of agreement and amens from the congregation. When the preacher raised his hands and intoned, "our dearly departed Sister Gussie," the choir faded and I could hear a man sobbing over the communal wail of anguish. I had never heard unashamed grief spoken out loud.

Peeking around the purple hat, I could see two women holding a stooped man by the elbows as he felt his way towards the coffin. He reached out both hands, wobbled forward and half fell across the open coffin. That must be Gussie's husband, I thought, and with a sudden shiver, hugged my arms tight across my chest. He's blind. I swiped at my dripping nose with the back of my hand, and was searching in my bag for a Kleenex, when the hat lady waved a packet of tissues over her shoulder almost hitting my chin. "I'm sorry," I whispered. "Thank you so much." I tore open the packet's cellophane with my teeth and blew my nose hard.

The women supported Mr. Preston back to his seat, and as if on cue, clusters of mourners started down the aisle toward the coffin. The woman in front of me rose and made her way forward, small boy in tow, hugging people as she went. Someone cleared his throat, and I looked up to see the usher inviting me to join the others. Mutely rude, I shook my head. I couldn't get up with all those people and file past Gussie's body. I'd told the lady I might have to leave early. Now's my chance. With my eyes down, I slid across the pew's cushions, pushed open the heavy church door and tiptoed into the jarring light.

Bitsy had worried about Gussie's husband ever since I told her about going to the funeral. "We should go visit him," she said with childlike simplicity. I hesitated. I had postponed thinking about him whenever thoughts of Gussie crept in. It would be embarrassing to call on a stranger, I reasoned. Even if his daughter was there, he wouldn't know who I was. It would be an imposition on a family in grief. And besides, I wouldn't know what to say. I didn't admit, even to myself, that this was a black family from another part of town.

"How can he take care of himself if he can't see?" Bitsy persisted.

At last, I summoned the courage to dial Gussie's number, my hand damp on the phone. A woman answered briefly. "Yes?"

Plunging on, I told her who I was and that I'd like to visit Mr. Preston. "Wait," she said. There were murmurs, then silence. I never should have called, I thought, hoping she'd tell me not to come. More murmurs, and the woman was back. "All right. Tomorrow, then. At 4:00 o'clock." The next day, with Rosie on one hip and Bitsy by the hand, we went to pay a call on Mr. Preston.

Rosie leaned to push the doorbell of the tidy house with its protective door grill like other houses on the short East Oakland block. A woman about Gussie's age opened the door a crack before she let us in, drying her hands on her apron. She was lighter skinned than Gussie and wore a scarf tied around the back of her head that reminded me of photographs of black women in the South. "I'm his sister," she said, adding her name so softly I couldn't hear and felt too shy to ask. She motioned towards the man folded into an armchair by a lace-curtained window.

"Your company's here," she said. Mr. Preston straightened to peer at us through filmy eyes. Except for some sparse furniture and a figurine on a side table, the room was as bare and immaculate as if Gussie had just finished "doing it up" with her Pine-Sol and mop. I wished fervently that I had thought to bring flowers. Mr. Preston held out his hand.

"Come a little nearer, please." His voice was unexpectedly strong. We crossed the dim room, and I shook his hand, greeting him loudly as if he were deaf as well as blind.

"This is Bitsy," I told him, and my daughter promptly put her small hand in his. "And this is Rosie." To my relief, Rosie peeked up from my shoulder and rewarded him with a tentative smile that I hoped he could see. He gestured toward the plastic-covered couch across from him.

"Please, won't you have a seat?" I sat stiffly forward, while Bitsy leaned back on one side of me swinging her Mary Jane sandals, and Rosie, on the other, kicked her toddler shoes back and forth in time to her sister's. The woman brought in a tray with three teacups, lemonade for the girls, and a bowl of vanilla wafers that she put on the coffee table in front of us.

Bitsy was pointing across at the fireplace. "Look, there's President Kennedy." Hanging above the mantel were two large pictures, one a painting of Jesus with a halo, and the other, a photograph of President Kennedy, the same size as Jesus. Mr. Preston's sister gave the girls their lemonade and handed me a cup of tea.

"Yes," she said, "That's our President Kennedy, God rest his soul, and that's our Lord Jesus Christ." She carried a cup to Mr. Preston, and took a straight-backed chair next to him. Bitsy stared at the pictures, Rosie reached for a second cookie, and I tried to think of something to say.

"It's good of you to come," said Mr. Preston in the same strong voice.

"I loved Gussie," I blurted, realizing for the first time that I did in fact love Gussie. I struggled to keep my mouth from trembling. "I'm so sorry," I managed. He nodded, smiling gently in acknowledgment.

"I guess everyone loved Gussie," he said. His sister said that Gussie had been buried in a military cemetery because Mr. Preston had been in the army, and I asked her where the cemetery was.

"It's a piece from here, on the way to Fresno. I don't like it she's gone so far, but it's the family plot."

She isn't hard to talk to, I thought. She's just shy, too. I asked Mr. Preston where he had been stationed. "Fort Hood, real hot," he said abruptly, and remembering the segregation in the army, I left the subject there.

Bitsy said, "No, thank you," when the sister asked if she'd like more lemonade, but Rosie held out her cup. I asked Mr. Preston how old his grandchildren were. "I don't rightly know." His forehead creased and he turned his head towards his sister for help. "Six and eight," she said.

"That's how old I am, six, almost seven," Bitsy volunteered. Rosie stopped swinging her feet and held up two earnest fingers. "Rosie's two," explained her sister.

Rosie pulled on my sleeve. "Home?"

"We should be going," I murmured to Mr. Preston, the way one does even when there's no reason to leave. He pushed himself up from his chair, and I wanted to put my arms around him. Instead, I held his dry hand in both of mine and thanked him for letting us come. "I'm glad for it," he said simply. "I hope you'll come again."

"Thank you. I'd like to." I hoisted Rosie onto my hip. "Can you say goodbye?" I whispered. She shook her head, but waved at him and Mr. Preston reached to pat her arm. He looked hazily down at Bitsy and held out his hand.

"Goodbye, Bizzy," he said.

She took his hand. "Gussie called me Bizzy too."

Out on the front porch, both girls broke away to hop madly up and down the sidewalk while I said a final goodbye. At the car, I turned to wave. The woman said something to Mr. Preston, and from the shadows behind the screen door's grill, they waved back.

A Visit to Berkeley

The traffic inched its way under the Flight Arrivals sign towards the San Francisco airport. Through the dim light, I could see my parents-in-law standing next to their maroon and navy monogrammed luggage. Mr. Holt held his hand in the air as if he were hailing a Fifth Avenue cab, and Mrs. Holt looked as polished as always in her coiffed grey hair and tailored traveling suit. If they were disappointed that we had moved to Berkeley, my in-laws never said as much. Instead, they came to visit every six months as regularly as the ticking of a metronome. Determined to make them proud of my home, their visits invariably brought me to my knees. Turning the playroom next to the kitchen into a presentable guest room was in itself a full day's job. I missed Gussie. I had never come close to imitating the Holts' immaculately appointed New York apartment with Moonie, their live-in maid.

As for Parks, his anxiety always went up a notch in anticipation of his parents' arrival. Sometimes, he was excessive in his admiration of their artistic talents and the movies they made of their trips around the world. Other times, he said he wished their plane would fall out of the sky. Once I heard him mutter from his closet, "What'll I put on? I don't know who I am." It reminded me of the night we went to see the movie, "Ordinary People" with Mary Tyler Moore playing the role of an unyieldingly cold mother. In a final scene, her son, looking for solace, had crawled into the lap of a stone statue of a seated woman. In the theater, I heard Parks's sharp intake of breath, and on the way home in the darkness of the car, I patted his shoulder while he wept.

Mr. Holt lowered himself into the backseat, and I remembered too late that I had forgotten to clean shedding hair from Mona Lisa, our basset hound, off the back seat. Mrs. Holt and I barely touched cheeks in an awkward imitation of a kiss. We were still recovering from my latest daughter-in-law blunder that I remembered all too well. Of my many faux pas, the paintings fiasco had been the worse.

Mrs. Holt was an accomplished watercolor artist, and understandably proud when she was elected to the coveted American Watercolor Society. Only last Christmas, she had sent three paintings to the kids: a horse barn in a field for Bitsy, lobster pots for Rosie, and a mountain trout stream for Mac. "I hope you will have them framed and hang them in the children's rooms," she wrote in her neat, straight-up-and-down script. But after my effusive thank you note in reply, it was a full month before I remembered to have them framed. Faithfully supporting new business, I chose a framing store that had only recently opened in our neighborhood. Together the young clerk and I picked out the frames. That much accomplished, I forgot the paintings again.

Two months later, a note arrived from Mrs. Holt. "Are the children enjoying the watercolors?" Dear God. I had completely forgotten their existence. With the three kids rocketing around in the backseat, it took me less than ten minutes to skid to a stop in front of the framing store. The windows were blank. On the sidewalk, I cupped my face to the glass.

"There's no one there," said Bitsy.

"The sign on the door says "Out of Business," said Mac, proud of his reading skills.

"I want out," demanded Rosie, left behind in the car. The room was empty, as lifeless as the day it was built except for a chair that lay sideways on the floor. No phone number. No forwarding address. No Lobster Pots, no Mountain Stream, no Horse Barn in a Field. The paintings had vanished into another world along with the store. My mother-in-law never answered my laborious letter of apology, and, to my relief, the subject was never mentioned again.

The first evening of their visit went surprisingly well except when a fillo dough crust under the broiler caught on fire and I yelled, "Goddammit-to-hell" from behind the kitchen door. During cocktails, my father-in-law whom we were all in the habit of calling Pa, was at his best reading Dr. Seuss out loud while the kids snuggled close to listen. They went to bed without complaint, and when Rosie dragged her worn-out blanket like a dust mop across the floor, Mrs. Holt, known now to everyone as Meme, graciously looked the other way.

Saturday morning, while I washed the breakfast dishes, Meme offered to help make a salad for lunch, and Rosie sat with her blanket on the counter to watch. "I don't like tomatoes, Meme," Rosie told her grandmother as Meme sliced one into a bowl.

"Of course you do," said Meme. "They're good for you."

"No, I don't," said Rosie firmly, rubbing her blanket binding against her cheek. She stared at her grandmother pensively. Meme stared back.

"Don't you think you're getting too old for a blanket?" she asked. Rosie's cheeks turned a shade pinker as confrontation loomed.

"Bitsy," I intervened, always anxious to avoid conflict. "Why don't you take Meme into the living room and show her your new books?" My daughter scrambled to her feet from where she was tying a bow on Mona Lisa's collar, and reached out her hand, sticky with orange juice and dog hair, to her grandmother. I could hear Parks's feet coming down the stairs and his father asking him how he was "getting along" in the department. Mr. Holt always wanted to know when his son was going to be promoted. I sighed. Parks was soon coming up for tenure at Cal where publish-or-perish was a reality. He had recently won the coveted departmental Distinguished Teaching

Award, but publishing theoretical criticism of original works was all that mattered. Fear of failure lurked constantly around the edges of our lives.

"Hey, in there," I called. "How about fixing your mom and dad a drink?" I had remembered to buy an expensive Dubonnet they liked before lunch, and was rummaging in the freezer for ice when Parks came in to pour the drinks.

"Is your dad on your case again?"

He shrugged. "You know how he is."

Rosie was watching me open a packet of shrimp to add to the salad.

"What's that?" she asked, wrinkling her nose.

"Shrimp."

"I don't like shrimp."

"You've never tasted shrimp, silly," teased her dad. He pretended to reach for her blanket. "Loan me your bankie, will you, Snoopy? I bet I need it more than you do."

Rosie giggled. "You're too old for a bankie, Daddy." Over lunch, while Bitsy took Rosie out to the sandbox and Mac played upstairs with his model trains, talk inevitably turned to politics. The campus was the focus of protests and riots against the Vietnam War, but absorbed in the care of my family, I had felt separate from what was happening. Even while the sound of helicopters floated overhead, I refined my tennis game on Rose Garden courts, a scant mile from where students broke windows on Telegraph Avenue and camped in People's Park. The Free Speech Movement, demonstrations and tear gas all went on around us, but from my sheltered life on the hill, they seemed to belong to someone else.

"I don't care what those people think about the war." Mr. Holt was saying. He always knew exactly what he thought. "They can't run around with their long hair like lawless hoodlums, breaking windows and vandalizing property! It's an outrage." Meme lit a cigarette before she had finished her salad, and I tried to think of a way to change the subject.

"But Dad," Parks protested. "The police are using clubs and tear gas on students and arresting them as if they were common criminals. A lot of them are only kids."

"Well, if they aren't criminals, what are they?" My father-in-law's fist hit the table making his salad plate bounce. "I tell you, there are enough problems in this world without a bunch of spoiled kids raising hell. I mean, look at the trouble we're having at home with your brother going to see a shrink, for God's sake." Fear caught in my throat and I glanced anxiously at Parks. Maybe something had happened to Devon. We knew that Parks's younger brother, who suffered from depression, had been stationed in Germany, but the Army had sent him home with a discharge for mental health. I wanted to ask more about him, but I didn't like to invade the circles of secrecy that surrounded the Holt family.

"Stop it, Parker! Just stop it," my mother-in-law spoke sharply to her husband. "We agreed we weren't going to talk about Devon and his problems." Pushing back her chair, she leaned to pick up one of two kittens left from a litter of four playing with a celery leaf on the floor and stroked its tiger back while it kneaded its tiny claws into the collar of her shirt.

"Well, what's the matter?" My father-in-law was defensive. "Devon will be fine once he connects a couple of wires in his brain. He just needs to learn how to have fun."

"Will you please just leave it alone?" Tears wet Meme's cheek. The only noise was the drone of the kitten's purr, unexpectedly loud in the silence of the room. Then she rose, put the kitten down on her chair and walked straight-backed through the kitchen into the playroom. The door closed behind her with a click.

I was starting to clear the salad plates when the girls' voices sang through the open front door. "Me-me, Me-me. Happy birthday to you, happy birthday to you." Rosie tiptoed towards the dining room carrying a muffin tin in each hand filled with sand and decorated with pink fuchsia blossoms. Mona Lisa, resplendent in her purple bow, nosed along behind in case anything edible dropped, and Bitsy brought up the rear.

Mac shouted down from the loft, "It's not Meme's birthday, silly."

Rosie scowled up at him. "It is too!" she insisted loudly, stepping squarely on a kitten's paw that let out a piercing screech and vanished under a chair. Muffin tins flew, scattering sand and fuchsia blossoms across the floor. Rosie sat down hard.

"My cakes! I want to give Meme my cakes." She dissolved into wails while her sister squatted to scoop up the sand. "She wanted to carry both of them by herself," Bitsy said apologetically, looking up at me.

"It's okay, Honey, it's not your fault. Thank you for helping." I put the stack of salad plates back on the table and gritted across the sandy floor to retrieve Rosie who would not be consoled.

"They were beautiful cakes, Rosie. Everything's fine. Meme just went into the playroom to take a little nap." I dabbed at Rosie's streaming nose with a paper napkin. "Guess what! There's a chocolate cake mix in the cupboard. Why don't we make some real cakes with candles and everything? Then when Meme gets up, we can have a party. Won't that be fun?"

Angie's Wedding

Our new cleaning lady was as robust and voluble as Gussie had been lean and taciturn. With dyed orange hair and snapping eyes, Angie landed in our midst like a cheerful brown bombshell. Angie loved to laugh. And Angie loved to talk. I heard stories about her neighborhood friends, their parties, and how they looked after each other's kids. By the end of her first day, I knew about her children (four), her mother (crazy), and her sister in Oklahoma (an alcoholic). By the end of her second day, I knew about her boyfriend (a gambler). "That man of mine, Lord, he makes me so mad the way he throws away his money gambling. But, oooh, is he good at loving. Just last night he was chasing me round the bedroom 'til I thought I'd die laughing." She thumped the iron on the collar of Parks's button-down shirt for emphasis, while I tried to imagine my husband chasing me around anywhere.

Both in our early thirties, I liked that Angie called me by my first name as if we were friends, and that she included me in the ongoing saga of her life. Sometimes she brought her baby to work if her cousin couldn't help out. She helped me feel connected to a community I hadn't found living in the hills where black families were rare, and children were scattered.

Angie had been with us nearly a year when she arrived pale, and full of troubles. "Me and the kids got evicted. That no-good man. He's gone and gambled away my rent money and my payments were three months overdue."

"Oh, Angie." It's not fair that I have things so easy, I thought, when life for others is so hard. She was staying with her cousin, and her kids were sleeping on the floor. What would it be like to be evicted from our home, I wondered, and where would we stay if we were?

Angie leaned on her mop. "I hate to ask, but do you think you and your husband could loan me a thousand dollars so I could catch up? I'm getting a tax refund in just a few weeks. Then I can pay you back."

A thousand dollars. I flinched. I'd never loaned anyone money like that. "Well, hmm, hold on, Angie, let me talk to Parker." I climbed the narrow stairs and knocked on the double doors of his study that shielded him from household noise. He was bent over a stack of papers, and I was surprised to see that his brown hair was thinning on top. Beyond his window, the afternoon sun slanted through trees into the canyon below.

When I told him about Angie's request, the line between his eyes deepened. "I don't think we should," he said slowly. "You know Dad always said not to loan people money if you want to be paid back. We won't see that money again."

"Angie said she could pay it back when she gets her IRS money, but even if she can't, it's not right that we don't have to worry when she can't make ends meet."

He shrugged. "I don't know. Do what you think is best." I went downstairs and wrote Angie a check.

Two months later, the crisis had blown over. Angie's man was back. She had forgiven him for his gambling and was running around the bedroom again. "Not only that," she said, holding out her left hand, "He proposed! And you have to come to the wedding. I want you and your family there." I was flattered. A black woman was inviting us to her wedding. Maybe the children could play together, and afterwards our families could visit back and forth. Be friends.

"Of course, we'll come. We wouldn't miss it."

But on the day of the wedding, Parks didn't want to go. He stood in the kitchen sipping a cup of tea and staring at the Bay. The fog was lifting, leaving a guarantee of fresh wind after the morning calm. "Look at this day," he said. "It's perfect. I want to take the boat out, and you and the kids could come."

86

My heart dropped. Parks had wanted to buy a sailboat and I had half-heartedly agreed. I knew how much he missed his childhood summers when he and his two brothers had had their own boat to play with in the inlets of New Jersey. He was happiest on the water. Maybe a boat on the Bay would help him feel more at home in California, the state I called my own.

Of course, the sailboat couldn't be just any boat. The Flying Spray was one-of-a-kind, complete with twenty-six feet of Philippine teak deck and rosewood trim that demanded special care. She was too big for Parks to manage comfortably alone, and sailing days for me were a challenge. When the kids were little, a sitter had to be found for the day. At the marina, thirty grommets on the custom-fitted cover had to be unfastened, engine primed, ropes coiled, gear stowed, cumbersome life jackets donned. It often took two hours of windless motoring towards Angel Island, gasoline smells wafting from below, before the breeze picked up and Parks scrambled to raise the sail.

"Pull hard on that rope."

"This one?"

"No, the aft one. The one nearest you."

"Parks, do you see that tanker? Over there by the bridge?"

"Tighter. Pull it to that cleat."

"I'm pulling"

Parks's eyes fasten to the top of the mast.

"Ready about?"

I'm never ready to come about.

"Coming about! Hard a-lee!"

Duck. Switch seats. Boom slams. Boat tilts alarmingly.

"How far away do you think it is?"

"What?"

"The tanker. Do you see how close it is?"

Cushions slide.

"Aft rope again. Good. Ready about?"

"I can see people on the bow. Do you think they see us?"
"Coming about! Hard a-lee!'"
Duck. Switch seats. Boom slams. Brace feet.

Finally back in Berkeley, salty and stiff, life jackets and cushions were stored, the last rope secured on the last cleat, decks hosed, cover hauled, and thirty grommets fastened into place. It had been a long day on the Bay.

The sinking feeling that Angie's wedding had turned out to be a "perfect day for the boat" gripped me. There was a pause while I summoned my nerve. "I can't," I said finally. "I promised Angie we'd come to her wedding. I don't want to let her down."

"What about letting me down?" My stomach clutched. I was disappointing my husband. I was refusing a day of sailing in favor of our cleaning lady's wedding. I knew he was hurt, but he rarely showed his anger and neither did I. That afternoon, Parks went morosely back to his study, Mac went to a friend's house, and Rosie, Bitsy and I went to Angie's wedding.

The address Angie had given me turned out to be a stucco bungalow in West Oakland near the Bay. "I thought the wedding was in a church," said Bitsy in disappointment.

"So did I," I said. "This must be her cousin's house." I pressed the buzzer and tried not to think about Parks alone in his study staring at the Bay. No one answered. Angie had said one o'clock. I rang again.

"Maybe she didn't hear," said Bitsy, banging hard on the door. After a few minutes, a girl about four, wearing a crisp yellow dress over wide petticoats opened the door an inch or two, enough to see us, but not to welcome us in.

"Hi," I said brightly. "Is your mama here?" Maybe Angie isn't her mama, I thought, and tried again. "Is Angie here?" The child disappeared from view.

"That was a pretty dress," said Rosie.

A voice. "I'm coming, I'm coming, don't pull me, girl." The door opened a foot, and Angie, clad only in a slip and backless slippers, stood looking at us in surprise, her face bland without makeup. "My goodness, you're here and look at me in my slip. I better hurry on up."

I wondered if she remembered she had invited us at all. "We can come back later, Angie, I thought it was one o'clock. It must be my mistake."

"No, no. Come on in." She looked at us doubtfully. "I hope you don't mind waiting a bit." Leaving us in the living room, she padded through the dining room past a lace-covered table with a tray of plastic glasses and cans of soda. The few folding chairs that had been added to a faded couch and a bunch of flowers on an upright piano were the only other signs of a wedding. Perched on one of the folding chairs, I had a sudden image of the sparkling Bay, and my hands felt cold with the realization that I might have made the wrong choice.

Bitsy and Rosie were asking if they could play double chopsticks on the piano when two boys about Bitsy's age appeared and started dancing to Motown 45's that dropped from a stack on their record player. They ignored Bitsy who stood back shyly to watch. The front door banged open and a preacher and a heavyset man nodded briefly at me before heading for the kitchen and the smell of frying chicken. The boyfriend, I thought, and wondered if he knew I had loaned Angie money. Other guests arrived and carried covered dishes towards the sounds of laughter in the back. If I'd thought to bring something, I scolded myself, I'd have an excuse to go to the kitchen too. Finally, a woman plumped herself down at the piano and began to pound out bridal chords. Guests came to take chairs near me as Angie, wearing false eyelashes and heavy makeup, appeared on the arm of the boyfriend. "Dearly beloved, we are gathered here together," began the preacher. Everyone sang hymns, and when the groom kissed the bride, the audience shouted its approval and made comments about what the couple would be doing later.

Afterwards, corks popped in the dining room and the girls and I sipped sodas while behind us, people clustered next to bottles of champagne. I knew how to stand around holding a glass of wine at faculty parties, but I didn't know how to join a group of strangers who were having such a good time together. Bitsy pulled on my arm. "Don't you think we could go now, Mommy? It's getting late, and Daddy's going to wonder where we are."

I put my arm around her, noticing again how much she worried about her father. "You're right, it's time to go." I found Angie in the kitchen. She looked as surprised that we were leaving as she had when we arrived. "Thank you for inviting us," I said politely. With an apology for not staying for fried chicken, we made our escape out the door, across the cement front yard and into the late afternoon. The sun was still warm as we drove home across Oakland city streets and into the familiar Berkeley hills.

A week after the wedding, Angie called to tell me that her family couldn't afford to live in Berkeley, and they were moving to Modesto to live with her husband's mother. She never paid the thousand dollars back, and I was grateful to Parks that he never said, "I told you so."

Decisions

It's hard to know exactly when a marriage begins to unravel.

In the mid-1970's, the Feminist movement was in full bloom. Betty Friedan had founded NOW, Gloria Steinem was trumpeting women's lib, and women everywhere were marching for the ERA. I watched it all while I took care of the house, chauffeured teenagers, and thought it daring to wear a long skirt and Birkenstocks to a faculty garden party. Thursday evenings on TV, I examined Mary Tyler Moore's every move, her clothes, her apartment, her job, and the way she talked to her boss, Mr. Grant. I got my ears pierced, volunteered at the kids' schools, and gave tennis lessons to other restless housewives on a neighbor's court. But that's not what Mary would have done. She would have found a real job. I refused to admit to myself that I wanted to be part of the women's liberation movement, that I needed to be liberated too.

The offer of a job at a private high school where Mac had thrived as a student for four years happened only by chance. Woodland Prep was a small, homey school that occupied one corner of a busy Oakland city block. Like other mothers who didn't work, I belonged to the Parents' Association and brought strawberries to afternoon teas. During Mac's senior year, I organized the school's fundraiser, and served on the Board of Trustees. Two months after graduation, Mac left for Princeton, sporting long hair and the tennis racquets he always carried as if they were an extension of his right arm. Rosie was admitted as a freshman to Woodland Prep that same fall, and Bitsy was a junior at a high school nearby.

At a reception for parents of new Woodland students, armed with an oatmeal cookie and a cup of punch, I found myself standing next to Mr. Cochran, the Headmaster. "What are you up to these days?" he asked politely. I liked him. Sandy-haired and sturdily straightforward with the familiar old-school-tie atmosphere he'd brought with him from the East Coast, he always looked as if he were on his way to an office on Wall Street.

"Not a lot," I admitted, and surprised myself by confessing, "I'm looking for something new to do." I glanced at Parks on the other side of the room leaning forward in tight-jawed conversation with someone I didn't know. He had been preoccupied for weeks about what courses he should teach in the fall quarter. Decisions were always hard for him. While the English department secretary waited to finish the course catalogue, Parks implored us to help him decide, changed and re-changed his mind, until his anxious paralysis left us all, including the kids, out of patience.

Mr. Cochran regarded me with a glint of interest. "I have an idea," he said, and stood looking at me for so long that I wanted to turn away. "I'd like to offer you a position that's opening up as the school's secretary and registrar. You'd be perfect for it." I blushed at the compliment. A real job. I'd love to do that, I thought. My head whirled. Taking care of the school's office sounded like fun, even exciting. I would be out of the house, making friends and doing something completely new. Across the room, Parks was still deep in conversation. Ever since his brother Devon died four years ago, I thought, he doesn't joke around and laugh the way he used to. The Holt family never mentioned the word suicide. They said Devon's death was accidental, but watching Parks, I felt a rush of panic. I remembered he said more than once that if something happened to me, he would take his own life. I was sure it was only a way of talking, but nonetheless, how could I think of being gone all day?

"Do you think the job could be part-time?" I asked.

Mr. Cochran shook his head. "Sorry, it has to be full-time. Five days a week with a month off in the summer." My enthusiasm ebbed. There was no way I could accept a full-time job, not to mention being away half of every summer. Parks would want me at home.

"Thank you, I really appreciate the offer," I said, "but I need time to talk about it with Parker. Can I let you know?" I knew the prospect was unlikely, but that evening, Parks and I discussed the pros and cons.

"There's the house to take care of and the girls to drive after school," he said. "And what about teaching tennis? You're great at that. Besides, there's the trip we promised to take with Mom and Dad next winter. They're counting on us."

"I guess you're right." It's logical not to rock the boat, I thought, but I wasn't quite sure why. He had a way of looking at me, with his brow knitted and his eyes fixed on my face that could persuade me of anything; we agreed it would be best for everyone in the family if I stayed at home. I called the school and turned Mr. Cochran's offer down.

But during the next couple of days, I couldn't stop thinking about the job. By the third day, I knew, with an unsettling determination, that I had made a mistake. I had let Parks talk me out of a chance to do something I might not have again. Why did I think that if I missed it, I would suffocate? Swept on a current of conviction that was out of my control, and without a word to Parks, I called the school. Mr. Cochran met me in the living room of the Yellow House, a clapboard relic of an old residence where teachers had their offices and ate lunch behind a vintage wisteria vine that climbed over the front porch. Classes were held next door in a drab cinderblock building that could have been a prison if it hadn't been built for a school.

Seated across from Mr. Cochran, I studied squares of afternoon light on the faded carpet. "I've changed my mind," I said, meeting his eyes with an effort. "If it's still available, I'd like to accept your offer after all." He leaned back, touched his fingertips together and gazed at me for a long minute over his half glasses in what I would learn was a characteristic pose whenever he pondered a response. "If you'll have me," I added.

"Are you sure?" he asked.

I nodded mechanically, trying not to think about Parks and how I was going to tell him when I got home. "I'm sure."

Another pause while he studied my face. "Then I look forward to having you on board," he said with a grin, getting up to shake my hand. Afterwards, I sat in my car, mindlessly watching the traffic, my hands cold. I should never have done it, I thought. If only I'd worked harder to make Parks happy, been more patient, more loving. How could I ever go home? But there was nowhere else to go. I forgot to breathe as I climbed the stairs to Parks's study. Maybe I'm having a heart attack, I thought, and inside his door, I leaned against his bookcase for support. He looked up at me, puzzled.

"I have to tell you something," I said. Motionless, he listened, his expression flat.

"But we made a decision."

"I know." I knotted and unknotted my hands.

"You didn't tell me."

"I know." I looked at the crease between his eyebrows that I was never able to smooth away.

His voice was even. "We were going to travel."

"We've just been traveling." I was defensive. To everyone's exquisite relief, the committee had finally promoted Parks to tenure, and to celebrate, we had toured Europe with the kids in a rented camper van for three months. We thought it a daring sabbatical, an adventurous escape from the tension of university life, but it had not been without a series of crises. The van had constantly broken down and we had to spend hours in gas stations negotiating blown gaskets with mechanics who spoke a language not our own. Decisions about where to go and when to stop were always problematic. One day, Parks had seen a display of different sized cowbells in the window of a hardware store. Enraptured by the sound of Swiss bells, he couldn't decide which one to buy. He debated, bought one, returned it, bought another, and took it back. Finally, while the kids and I waited on the sidewalk, awkward and embarrassed, his dilemma was so extreme that, to the clerk's bewilderment, he ended up buying all six.

"We can still travel in my time off," I offered lamely. Four weeks of vacation seemed like plenty of time to me. Wordlessly, he picked up his glasses and turned his back. I thought about Mr. Cochran's question, Are you sure? and felt another rush of panic that I had let my husband down. My hands on his shoulders, I kissed the top of his head. "I'm sorry," I said gently.

"Classes start in a couple of weeks," he said without looking at me. "I have to write a syllabus." He'll come round, I thought, trying to reassure myself as I went downstairs, my legs still shaking from fear. He'll see that this job will be good for me, that it will add interest to our life together. But a boulder of silence settled on the house. For days his door remained closed and he came down from his study only when he had to, looking stony-faced at meals. One afternoon when I was in the garden, I saw him watching me out the window. Another time, I thought he might be crying. I was conflicted with a mixture of guilt, anger and resolve. Was I the one who let this happen? Was he really this dependent on me?

But I went anyway. On the first day, my heart pounding in my ears, I left Parks standing dismally at the door. With Rosie in the seat next to me and Genty, our golden retriever, in the back, I drove to Woodland Prep to start my full-time job.

From the beginning, I felt at home. With only a hundred students, a small faculty, and Deena Jones, cook for the faculty and surrogate grandmother who reminded me of Gussie, I had added a new family to my own. This was where I belonged.

Every morning, Deena sighed her way into the school in her carpet slippers, wearily pushing an overloaded shopping cart past scruffy freshman boys shooting baskets under trees. I could hear her scolding at them. "You help me with these bags right now, you hear me?" Later, smiling in spite of herself, she leaned out the kitchen doorway, bantering with students and holding out a dish of sweets.

The office, the size of a rabbit warren, was the focus of the school's tiny universe. And I loved it. A large bay window kept the school's comings and goings in view, and in the winter, I didn't mind when rainwater seeped down the wall behind my desk and people streamed in and out the door. I felt important while I listened, comforted, and problem-solved across piles of typing and registrar work that filled my desk. Mr. Cochran accepted Genty as school mascot without a murmur of surprise. Wearing a *Please Don't Feed Me* sign on her collar, she earned her keep by mooching around for food and exuding an air of fuzzy comfort. After lunch, she slept behind my desk where Mr. Cochran was always careful to say, "I'm sorry, Genty," each time he stepped across her to reach a file drawer. Poor Parks, I thought with a stab of guilt, I didn't even leave him the dog.

Being the Head of School is filled with challenges, and I watched Mr. Cochran handle worried families and resolve difficult situations without looking back. "Life is rich and full," he liked to say with a rueful twinkle in his eye. Rarely was he more upset than that. But at home, Parks's painful inability to make decisions ruled our lives. He kept a carpenter waiting for days when he couldn't decide on the width of the posts for a new fence. Another time, the university administration changed its pension plan and asked faculty members to choose between two retirement packages. Parks was frozen into immobility. Finally, on the last afternoon, Bitsy and I had to make the decision for him. I don't remember which one we finally picked, but I do remember that in the long run, it hadn't mattered.

His chronic depression deepened and a general gloom settled into the corners of the house. I began to put off going home. It was more fun to stop by the office of the school's elderly bookkeeper on a Friday afternoon where, armed with a wicked sense of humor, she was always up for a laughing good gossip over a glass of sherry from the bottle she kept in her bottom drawer. At home, with a mixture of sympathy and frustration, I listened to Parks's worries about what to teach and what to write; he listened to stories I brought home from school, but with a distant look in his eyes. The girls felt the heaviness too. I wished Mac were not so far away, but even when he was home from college where he was on the tennis team, I couldn't blame him for wanting to spend much of his time practicing for tournaments or being with his friends. My family's edges were unraveling, and I didn't know how to sew them back together.

"Let's move," I said once, with an enthusiasm I didn't feel. "Wouldn't you be happy teaching in a high school? We could try something completely new." An old idea, but worth another try.

He only shook his head. Bitsy graduated from high school, changed her name to Liz, and left a hole in our lives when she left for the University of Oregon. At the local bank, I opened a small savings account I privately called my Runaway Fund, and unabashedly flirted with the teller, attracted by his laugh lines and the deep humor in his eyes.

Rosie was in her senior year, when Parks came to me before I left for work. Would I ask Mr. Cochran if Parks could apply for a job as Woodland's school librarian? I stared at him in dismay. Was he kidding? Woodland's library consisted of a series of bookshelves at the back of the auditorium carefully tended by self-effacing Mrs. Booth. "I can't do that for you," I started to say, but stopped. The depth of his dejection took my breath away. Later, in my boss's office, I shifted in my chair with embarrassment.

"Here? He wants to be the librarian here?" Mr. Cochran asked.

"Yes," I admitted miserably.

"Isn't he a full Professor of English at UC?"

"Yes."

"We already have a librarian."

"I know."

Mr. Cochran leaned back, touched his fingertips together, and gazed at me for a long minute over his half glasses. At last, with a hint of sympathy in his voice, he said, "I don't think that's a good idea. Do you?"

"No," I said. "I don't."

Parks started therapy, and before long he insisted I go as well. The psychiatrist, a broodingly handsome man, was one of those shrinks who regards his patients with a bemused expression and says nothing. With one leg folded under him, he lounged in a leather rocker, while rigid, we faced him side by side in wicker chairs. I spent the time inching my chair slowly backwards until I was out of Parks's line of sight unless he craned his head, a process the therapist observed with only a slight quirk at the corner of his mouth.

I found a therapist of my own. At the end of our first meeting, she said gently, "You are carrying burdens that are far too big for you to handle. If you want, you can leave them here until you're ready to pick them up again." I stared at her with an overwhelming sense of relief that someone besides me thought that what I was doing was hard. Session followed session, while gradually, in minute increments, the idea of actually leaving my marriage crept into the back of my mind.

Rosie was accepted at Stanford, and the summer after her high school graduation, I heard about a rental at the top of the hills behind the Berkeley campus. A tree-shaded cabin was available for nine months while the owner led the first all-woman team on a climbing expedition to Nepal. I'll only take it for a little while, I thought, but deep in my heart, I knew I wouldn't be back. "A woman's place is on top," the mountain climber told me as she handed me the keys.

One September afternoon in 1981, Rosie left for Stanford, and with a mixture of heartache and disbelief, I packed my suitcase. "I'm going to be away," I told Parks, averting my eyes from his face. "I need some space." With the family parakeet chirping nervously on the back seat, and faithful Genty bolt upright in front, I left to climb a mountain of my own.

I didn't know how else to leave.

An Interlude With Charles

My romantic notion of being a liberated woman spreading her wings into a new life did not last long. I soon discovered I had no idea how to fly. At first, I relished the cabin on the hill with its deck reaching into the woods, the sound of the rain on the roof that first wet winter when rivers ran down the road. I delighted in a new neighbor, curly haired young Lily who moved into a tiny cabin behind mine and transformed it into a Tahitian hideaway. We ran together across miles of the Skyline fire trail before work while she entertained me with details of her affair with a married businessman across the Bay. "Last night we did it in a phone booth," she told me once as we panted through a dripping dawn under pungent-smelling bay trees. It was an effort for me to imagine such an acrobatic feat.

As winter deepened, the cabin began to seem empty after the life I had had with my family. Evenings were lonely, and I often woke in the night frightened for Parks by himself in the house down the hill. The kids spent time with their dad, but they were busy living their own lives. Mac was in his first year of law school in San Francisco; Rosie was engulfed by Stanford and its challenges; Liz was finishing her degree at UC Davis. It would be a year before Parks and I agreed to sell the house, but I knew that if I saw him again, his dejected expression alone would persuade me to come back. It didn't take me long to fill the void with the secure familiarity of another man.

Charles and I had been casual tennis friends for years. Divorced and from an affluent Seattle family with a sternly hard-edged stepfather and a Christian Scientist mother, Charles was fifteen years older than I. He had an exuberance for life so in contrast with Parks that I soon began to look at our tennis friendship with new eyes. I thought him strong and manly with his aristocratic beak of a nose, bristling eyebrows over twinkling eyes, and knotted forearms. And, most importantly, like me, he had a passion for writing and art. After work, I could find him in his crowded backyard studio where he was writing a book about tennis, surrounded by mugs of idle tea as he crouched over his computer, running one hand through unruly hair while he wrote, oblivious to the contents of his life that spilled around him at random. In spite of a rigidity to his religion and politics, he was fun. He liked to tease. "Is that you, Molly?" he joked when he heard me outside his door. Or "Charles isn't here! Are you looking for Randolph?" In free afternoons, we played tennis together in sharply competitive doubles at the Berkeley Rose Garden courts. I envied his eagerness to use every moment of his existence fully, with no concern that he should be using it any other way.

When the cabin rental on the hill came to an end, I threw away my hard-earned independence and moved in with Charles. I tried to ignore that he was a devoted Christian Scientist and a down-to-the-bone Republican, and that his low-ceilinged house was not far from where I had raised my family with Parks. In no time, I had succumbed to the familiar safety of sharing a bed, cooking dinners, vacuuming floors and keeping the counters clean. I didn't stop to wonder where this might be going, or where it might end.

Charles accepted my domestic contributions as a matter of course, but he was the first man to tell me I could be anything I wanted to be. After eight years, I quit my job at Woodland Prep, and thinking I wanted to become a school counselor, enrolled in a local graduate psychology program. Charles encouraged me to indulge my growing interest in photography in his downstairs darkroom. I began experimenting with black and white film, and when I added a weekly photography class and joined a writing group, I knew that the shell of the egg that had been me was beginning to crack open.

It was my father who had first introduced me to a darkroom. During the two years he spent convalescing from tuberculosis before I was born, he had to give up a career in nuclear physics in which dramatic advancements during those years had left him behind. To fill the space, he had taken up amateur photography. I had grown up with his portraits and landscapes along with volumes of famous photographers like Dorothea Lange and Margaret Bourke-White. When we were young, Annie and I spent Christmas vacation evenings helping print the annual family greeting card in his makeshift darkroom where developing pans were spread on Auntie B's ironing board. The alluring sound of the softly whirring exhaust fan mixed with the acrid tang of chemicals and ghostly red light gradually crept into my soul.

On vacations, Charles and I traveled to Northwest beaches where I photographed gnarled wood and weathered rocks, and we played tennis on public courts in the rain. On longer trips, we visited his daughter in Italy and pretended we were serious art students in every museum we could find. But like hidden fissures in the rocks I photographed, I began to run into crevices in Charles that ran deep. For a while it didn't matter that he was a devout Christian Scientist who fully embraced a religion I stubbornly refused to accept. But it became harder to ignore his politics, to turn silently away from his dogmatic convictions and overbearing insistence that Reagan was our finest president. Again, I longed to live alone.

"And besides, Mom," my daughter Liz pointed out with her characteristic clarity when she made one of her visits from school where she was finishing her degree in agriculture. "You lived twenty-five years of married life with a man in a redwood house in the hills. You've always said how much you wanted to be independent, and now you're living with another man in a redwood house in the hills. Think about it."

While I thought about it, my life took a dramatic change. My sister Annie was diagnosed with lung cancer. She was fifty-two.

A Summer Called Annie

In the doctor's cramped examining room, Annie sat on the edge of the papered table, hands gripped on either side as if she might fall off. She had asked me to go with her to have a persistent pain in her shoulder checked, and now fear shivered down my spine. I stood next to her, trying to make sense of the X-ray the doctor held against a lighted screen.

"Are you sure?" I asked the doctor. "There must be some mistake."

"Do you see where the tumor is?" He pointed at the X-ray. "It extends from behind the left lung here and into the shoulder." He stared at the wall behind Annie, unable, or unwilling, to meet her eyes. "It's big, way behind the lung, an inoperable form of lung cancer. We can try to slow it down, but we can't cure it." Immaculate in his white coat, he had wasted no time. No emotion, no fuss, just the facts.

"I know." Annie sounded flatly accepting, as if she had guessed it was cancer all along.

"We'll start with radiation which should shrink it for a while and then we'll see about chemotherapy." He wrote directions on a slip of paper in the undeipherable cribbed handwriting doctors always use. "Make an appointment with my nurse to see me in a few weeks." With a nod to me, and a pat on the hand for Annie, he was out the door.

Silently we made our way to the car where we sat together while she lit a cigarette and I tried to understand. This can't be happening, I thought. Death happens in other families. Not in ours. "My God, Annie! The doctor must be wrong. We have to do something."

"Now, listen here," she said, exhaling into the windshield as she turned onto Telegraph Avenue. "He's the head oncologist.

You saw the X-rays. I want this to be treated like it's no big deal." Out the car window, I watched an old lady hobbling towards a bus and waving her cane as it pulled away from the stop. I was glad when the driver waited, his blinkers flashing.

We both came from a family where emotions were kept private and it was considered an embarrassment to cry. Annie had always kept herself especially tight to the mast, but I couldn't imagine ever saying that cancer was "no big deal." Absorbed in the details of my own life and my divorce only two years earlier, I had paid scant attention to what was going on with my older sister. She had moved to Berkeley a few years after Parks and me, bought a small house on the other side of town, acquired a poodle, and settled into a job as an office manager at the university. Never married, she filled her role as an auntie to my children and a gruffly loyal sister to me.

Our reserve towards each other had grown out of an earlier time. Long before I was born, when my brother Thad was only four and Annie was a baby of six months, my father had become seriously ill with tuberculosis. In a time when there were no antibiotics or vaccinations, bed rest in a sanitorium for those who could afford it was the only known treatment. In the winter of 1934, Mother and Dad had made the difficult decision to leave the two children in New Haven with their grandmother in her three-story house. Together they made the long train trip to the Trudeau Sanitorium in upstate New York.

I grew up listening to stories of that painful time. Mother liked to sit next to me on the couch in the study at 596, a photograph album spread across our laps. She turned the pages with their black and white pictures of the imposing New Haven house and of handsome little Thad and baby Annie, her head covered with white-blonde curls. Their expressions were large-eyed and watchful. Mother always paused dramatically in her story. "It was such an exciting time to be at Princeton where Daddy was doing a postdoctoral fellowship in physics. I remember seeing Einstein striding across the campus in a cap and gown." She gazed out the window. "But one terrible night, we woke up and Daddy was coughing up blood. It was even on his pajama shirt. Can you imagine? I was scared to death."

What must it have been like, I wondered, to live in terror of a disease where the life of a beloved husband felt the same as personal survival? And what was it like for the children left behind? "It broke my heart to leave them," Mother sighed. "But what was I to do?" I couldn't imagine leaving my own children, but I knew that in those days, the damaging effect on very young children separated from their parents was little understood.

"I don't know," I always said, because I didn't. And what must it have been like, I wondered, for my Victorian grandmother to be suddenly saddled with two children for months at a time? I remembered her as an aged lady, whose wispily unassuming exterior belied strong opinions on such matters as galoshes and Vicks Vapor Rub. The children had probably been put in the care of maids. And what must it have been like for my father to be pulled away from a promising career in nuclear physics by a debilitating illness?

It took nearly two years, with only occasional visits back and forth to New Haven, for my father to slowly heal. But recover he did, and to everyone's surprise, I was conceived during their time away. "I was hor-ri-fied," Mother beamed at me. "Can you believe I repeatedly jumped off the rumble seat of our car in hopes of dislodging you? But there you were, born at the sanitorium! Thank God I didn't succeed!" She pointed at a photograph of a dark-haired baby in her arms, smiling up at her and clapping dimpled hands. What was it like, I always wondered, for my brother and sister to have their parents back, but with a baby sister to contend with as well? We had played together as children, but Annie always carried an edge of resentment, and I, a vague, but unrelenting guilt. Sometimes I wondered if I should have been born.

Glancing at Annie's profile as she drove, it was hard to tell if her hair had some blonde or if it had turned completely gray. Her narrow forehead and prominent nose reminded me a little of my dad, but a lifetime of smoking and cocktails had thickened her body and she looked older than her years. We had been raised around cigarettes and were used to Mother's yellow-stained ashtrays or a half-smoked cigarette in its black holder balanced on the edge of the kitchen sink. I didn't mind; it was part of who my mother was. I can still remember the sickly sweet tobacco smell of her handkerchief fished from the recesses of her purse to wipe our sticky mouths. I learned to smoke in college, but gave it up when my children, riveted by TV anti-smoking ads, demanded, "Mom, why are you doing something that's going to make you die?" I went cold turkey and threw half a carton of L&M's into the garbage. There's nothing lonelier than five packs of cigarettes lying in the bottom of a rain-drenched can.

"It's like a mortuary down here," Annie grumbled in the hospital's radiation department waiting room that made me think of a bomb shelter. Three other patients watched her fill out medical forms on a dimly lit waiting room table covered with thumbed copies of Sports Illustrated. I had a sinking feeling as we stared at the form's blank line: Primary Care Person. Who was there in the family to help? I thought about my brother Thad back in Brooklyn, immersed in his teaching job and his responsibility for his beloved wife in remission from breast cancer. I thought about Mother and Dad hundreds of miles away in Altadena. Traveling was harder for them as they turned eighty, especially for Mom, whose anxiety about everything had increased with age. They certainly couldn't come.

"I guess Primary Care Person means me," I said, and Annie scribbled down my name, adding (sister) and the date, June 1, 1985.

"You're lucky to have a sister," said the nurse.

"I know," said Annie, and I felt a flood of warmth.

Late spring disappeared into summer and time ground on in a blur of doctor visits, mashed bed pillows, reruns of *I Love Lucy*, and banks of fog rolling in through the Golden Gate. The cancer tightened its grip. Still living with Charles, I visited Annie every day, drove her to appointments, bought flavored Ensure she said tasted like wet Kleenex, cleaned the litter box in a kitchen that smelled of Tuna-4-Cats, and wrote and re-wrote the medications chart. If I just work hard enough and do my job well enough, I thought, I can make this nightmare end. That's what Primary Care people do. Through it all, I rarely sat down, and never thought to stop, to hold my sister's hand and say, "I love you."

The oncologist said Annie's tumor wasn't responding to radiation, and prescribed a course of intensive chemotherapy to begin the following week. But one intravenous dose of metallic chemo in the hospital made her violently ill. "The hell with it. I'm done with this. That goddamn doctor should take some of this crap himself so he'd know what kind of shit-poison he put in my veins."

It was time for me to leave Charles and move in with Annie. "Marry me," he said. But I couldn't and I didn't. The next week Genty and I settled onto a futon on Annie's dining room floor. To our credit neither Charles nor I wanted to give up the things that we had shared, and we remained loyally supportive friends for the rest of his life. He encouraged me to bring Annie for visits on sunny afternoons on his patio, and endeared himself to me by overcoming his disapproval of mind-altering drugs, and baking marijuana muffins in an unsuccessful effort to relieve her chronic nausea and pain.

Annie's office colleagues came and went, and one devoted friend brought her dinner twice a week so I could go to class. Late one night, I saw her light was on. Her eyes were closed, hair matted against the pillow, her body still. The bedroom smelled of cats. I stood watching her, frightened by a look of death. If she died, she would be free, I thought, and realized with sudden panic that for a moment I'd wished she had. A train whistled near the Bay. "Annie. Are you all right?"

She opened her eyes. "What are you doing up?" Her voice, irritable, had become a grating whisper behind teeth chipped by cancer. Or radiation. Or both. "Go back to bed. You'll be worn out." Ignoring her, I pulled a book off her shelf, and sat down next to her.

"How about I read aloud?"

"Well, I don't know what I think about that," said Annie in her customary refrain, but paying no attention, I began to read *A Town Like Alice*. Every night after that, under a single lamp, with Annie's poodle curled on her bed and Genty at my feet, we made an island of two in a world that slept. Night after night, we suffered the heroine Jean Paget's trials during the war, admired her strength, and rejoiced in her love for Joe Harman. Over time, Annie's testiness ebbed into a sweetness I hadn't seen before and a new ease of being settled between us.

We took a brief intermission from illness to celebrate Mac's wedding, and I took it upon myself to organize the rehearsal dinner at a nearby inn. The next day, I watched the wedding through a window of fatigue, and later, I had to look at photographs to remember it at all. There was the traditional church and the lovely bride, a classmate of Mac's at law school. There was a photograph of my handsome son with his Tom Selleck moustache next to my attractive bridesmaid daughters, and one of Parks with his eyes on me, transparent in their misery. There were photos of an evening party awash in champagne, and lastly, a snapshot of Annie in front of the church, thin as a rail, smiling bravely up from a wheelchair. The day after the wedding, Charles generously invited the family to a post-wedding breakfast in his house where I had once lived. But when the weekend was over, everyone went home, leaving Annie and me alone.

One late October evening, a sudden attack of vertigo flipped my world upside down. Throughout the night, the room spun in circles and I vomited on the floor whenever I moved my head. As the window above me greyed into morning, I heard Annie rasping something into the phone next to her couch. There was a knock on the door, paramedics' voices, and Annie's croaking whisper, "No, no, it's not me, it's my sister. Over there, on the floor."

At the hospital, whenever I woke through a haze of valium, Charles was there, sitting with his newspaper near my bed. What's a Christian Scientist doing in a hospital, I wondered foggily, as I drifted back to sleep. When it was time to go back to Annie's, my doctor was insistent. "You are going to stop trying to take care of your sister by yourself." The next day, Adelaide arrived from an agency. Her skin was a rich black, her uniform was white, her shoes squeaked and her hair lay in cornrows that must have taken hours to braid. She got right to work, organizing medicines, writing Annie's temperature on a chart and serving her lunch on a tray with a folded linen napkin unearthed from a kitchen drawer.

"Well, I don't know what I think about that," muttered Annie. The comforting smell of Pine-Sol and the feeling she gave me that everything was going to be all right reminded me of Gussie.

"She's so nursie," Annie complained after the first day.

"I think she's sent from heaven," I said, and we left it at that.

"I sing in the Hawkins Gospel Choir at the Love Center," Adelaide told me. "Why don't you bring your sister down to hear us one time soon? She would be welcomed by the Lord."

I glanced back at Annie whose hair, backlit against the window, did give her a slightly ethereal look. She was shaking her head at me and mouthing, "No."

"That's very kind of you," I said awkwardly. "Maybe soon." Adelaide was too polite to complain when Genty pressed a damp nose against her skirt or the poodle yapped at her feet. But in the middle of her second week, she motioned me into the kitchen. "I apologize, but I have to give notice."

"Oh, no, Adelaide, you can't. Have we done something wrong?"

"It isn't you or your sister, but I'm allergic to fleas. Their bites are making me crazy."

Fleas? I hadn't noticed. It was true the cats had been scratching. "I'm so sorry, Adelaide, I had no idea."

She took a notepad from her purse and wrote down her phone number. "Here's how to reach me in case you ever need me. You know what I'm saying?"

"Yes," I said, "I do," and stuck the paper into the back of my wallet. "Oh, dear," I sighed aloud after she left.

"It's just as well," said Annie. "Agencies send people like that. Too religious."

The next week, we hired Heidi, a friend of a friend, a red haired young nurse from Switzerland wearing jeans and an easy grin. "I can't work nights," she said, "but I can help you out during the day." As the cancer advanced, Annie didn't mind when Heidi took charge, soothed, laughed and persuaded the doctor to up the morphine dose. When Annie gave up trying to lie on the couch, Heidi and I moved a rented hospital bed in its place where she could look down the curving street, beyond a telephone pole to a bit of the Bay.

The day after Thanksgiving, walking into the bathroom, Annie's thighbone snapped. At the hospital, they slid a rod into her leg to hold it together and sent her home. Two weeks later, she had a seizure and was back in the hospital, this time in a room that was spaciously windowed. The cancer has gone into her brain, they said, and that evening, a new doctor listened to her chest while she slept. "There is pneumonia in both lungs. I'm prescribing intravenous antibiotics," he shrugged, as if to say, "It's too late anyway." I was left alone with Annie and my exhaustion. The silence in the hall was broken only when somewhere in the distance, a doctor was paged and someone's phone rang. I can't leave Annie alone, I thought, with sudden clarity. Even in the hospital, she has to have one of us with her. Heidi can only be here part of the time, and I can't stay all night. I wiped tears with the back of my sleeve. "I don't think I can do this any more," I said out loud.

Then I remembered Adelaide's paper in my wallet, and dialed her number on the pay phone down the hall. "And how is that sweet lady, your sister?" Adelaide spoke as if three months hadn't passed. "Yes, of course I can come. Honey, you are not alone. God is with you always." Tears welled again. It was a prayer for me. In less than an hour, Adelaide, pristine as ever in her uniform, put her head in the door while behind her, a black man wearing round spectacles and a minister's collar under a sweatshirt loomed. "I brought the Reverend, my husband," she said. "We knew your sweet lady would want to have our prayers."

"Well, I don't think so," I started, but the Reverend's arms were around me and I relaxed against him, muffling tears into the burly comfort of his sweatshirt, rough from many washings. At Annie's bed, he spoke to her tenderly. She's getting prayers whether she likes it or not, I thought, and half expected her to sit up and announce, "I hope you're not trying to save me!"

Adelaide stayed three nights. One crystal December morning, it was just getting light when my phone rang. Adelaide's voice was a whisper.

"Your lady has taken a turn for the worse."

"Will I be in time?"

"Yes."

I called Heidi, and with a cup of coffee in hand, drove past lampposts festooned with Christmas wreathes and one lonely car with a tree tied on top. From the windows of Annie's room, early sun was turning the Bay a luminous blue and reflecting on windows in San Francisco like beacons of gold. A nurse in a flowered smock came and went checking machines, while Adelaide, Heidi and I took turns holding Annie's cool hands, her chest rasping slightly in and out.

Suddenly, the door opened and a man slipped quietly into the room. Slender in jeans and sandals, his delicate features were radiant as if he were there to greet old friends. I put out my hand to stop him. "Who are you? You're in the wrong room."

"No, I should be here. My name is Michael. I've come to see Annie."

"But you can't. She's dying." My voice was shrill.

He held up two fingers in a sign of peace. "I know. Adelaide told me. I go to her church." Too taken aback to stop him, I followed him to Annie's bed where Adelaide hugged him and he held Annie's face softly with both hands, speaking to her in her coma as if they were having a conversation.

"How did you know to come here this morning?" I asked. This was too weird.

"I volunteer at an AIDS hospice in the city. That's my calling." His eyes smiled into mine. "People say I'm psychic. I heard someone mention the name Annie on television this morning and I knew it was time." With his hand gentle on my back, we made an oddly surreal circle around the bed: a gay psychic in sandals, a gospel singer in a nurse's uniform, a Swiss

114

nurse in overalls, and me. I could hear Annie's voice. "This is going to be no big deal."

Her breathing quieted, and we watched the lines and numbers on the machine above her head slow, slow some more, and then come to a stop. The flowered nurse looked at the clock, I looked at Heidi and back to Annie. A sense of disbelief and unreality overwhelmed me, as if I were far away, looking down on strangers frozen in space. How could months of illness, months of care, months of pain, months of waiting suddenly be over? I was not prepared for the finality. A social worker appeared by my side holding a clipboard and pen. She wanted me to sign something. How could this have happened, I wondered, reaching automatically for her pen. How could Annie be gone?

Annie would have said it was "no big deal" when, a year later I took her ashes down from the top shelf in her dining room and quietly buried her in the garden where freesias bloomed white and yellow along the edge. The garden that was now mine. Annie had left me her house.

The Y That Wasn't

Not long after I had settled into Annie's house, I went for a run in an early spring rain. Stopped for a traffic light, I surprised myself by suddenly shouting through the mist, "I want to make a difference," as if I were finishing a conversation with God. A difference doing what? I had no idea. Finally, energized by my own epiphany and the coincidence of an imminent presidential election, I threw myself into political activism.

Michael Dukakis was not a particularly compelling candidate, but my habitual enthusiasm for defeating a Republican, any Republican, inspired me. No one was surprised when he lost to George Bush, but it wasn't because I hadn't spend months working in a local Dukakis office. Later, in despair at the Persian Gulf War and enthralled by Thich Nhat Hahn's writings on peace and meditation, I bought a zafu and learned to sit cross-legged for longer than I thought possible. I joined the Berkeley Buddhist Peace Fellowship, marched silently every week in Oakland, and for a few Friday afternoons joined like-minded Buddhist wannabes sitting under a NO MORE WAR banner on the Berkeley university's front lawn. But it was my passion for the pro-choice movement during the Bush presidency that carried me to the Women's March in Washington D.C.

The cab pulled to a stop in front of a row of darkened faceless buildings and the driver craned to look at me over his shoulder. His lips pursed with concern. "Lady? It ain't my business, but you sure this is where you want to go?" The plane had been late and the time on his dashbord shone 10:40 p.m. Washington time.

117

"I'm sure," I said firmly. "This is where I'm staying. At the Y. They're expecting me. I'm here for the march," I added unnecessarily.

A friend, Leanne, had invited me to go with her to the demonstration. Because she was a travel agent, she could pick up half price deals at hotels where guests luxuriate in thick white robes, and room service is delivered by a staff that understands the discreet line between being a servant and being a friend.

"I have a pass to the Washington Hilton," she said, "Let's go together and we can hobnob with the rich. It'll be fun."

"Thanks," I told her, "I'd love to go to the march with you, but I'd rather stay at the Y. I can meet more women that way."

"Suit yourself," she replied in her usual upbeat way.

The cab waited while I climbed concrete steps to a shredding welcome mat. In the dim light from the street, I could make out a "YWCA" etched on a corroded brass plaque next to the door and gave the waiting driver a confident thumbs-up sign before pressing the bell. No response. The cab disappeared around the corner and I pressed the bell again. "Yeah?" I started at a sudden voice from the half opened door. A woman's silhouette, a stern, ghost of a figure, was backlit by a shaded green lamp on a desk behind.

"Umm. I have a reservation. I called two weeks ago. This is the Y, isn't it?" I hoped I sounded friendly, but competent. The woman, shapeless in a housedress and sweater held across her chest by uneven buttons, opened the door far enough to let me in. Sliding the bolt behind me, she retreated to the desk, her eyes narrow with suspicion.

"Used to be the Y. Now we house women. Take in a few outsiders. It helps pay. How long you be here for?"

"At least a couple of days. I'm here for the march." The floor upstairs creaked and she pointed towards the stairs.

"You can use Room 3, one flight up, three doors down on the right. There's a pay phone at the end of the hall."

I looked around. There was no talk and laughter in a cozy common room where I had imagined interesting women would be sitting together drinking tea. "Will there be a place to get coffee?"

"No ma'am, we don't make coffee. Most folks make do with a hot plate, but you can go to the deli, two blocks down. They got coffee." She snapped off the lamp.

I picked up my suitcase, conscious of the woman's eyes following me up the stairs. At the top, there was one light bulb and a red exit sign at the end of the hall. Probably a fire escape, I thought, and wondered if I'd have to drop to the ground at the bottom or if there would be a ladder. A woman, holding the pay phone close, put her hand over the receiver when she saw me, but when I raised my arm to wave, she turned her back and went on talking. While I fumbled with my key, a woman, skinny in a faded batik wrap, came out of Room 4. Our eyes met briefly. If she was surprised to see me there wearing my best PTA mother smile, she didn't let on. She trailed past me carrying a bar of soap and holding a towel to her mouth. From the bathroom the sound of running water and a heavy cough.

Room 3 was bare except for a bureau missing a knob and a steel frame bed with a blanket folded at one end. I sank down on the bed in lonely dismay, got up again, and with some effort, shoved the solid bureau in front of the door. That's stupid, I thought, who would try to get in? My familiar flannel nightgown was comforting as I curled fetal position onto the narrow bed next to the wall I shared with Room 4. Before long, through the wall, the woman's cough started deep in her lungs and hacked its way painfully to the surface and she spit out phlegm. A short relief, and it started again. In unison we dozed, when in unison she and I woke to her cough, a rasping air hammer in the night. Was that what Dad had sounded like at the tuberculosis sanitorium? Thus we passed the time until daylight seeped under the window blind and my watch read a little after six. We had made it through the night.

Images of richly steaming coffee swam before me as I made my way to the mercifully empty bathroom. Back on the bed, I wondered when the deli down the street might open. Their coffee would be horrible. Next door, there was another desolate cough. I should stay here and help the woman in Room 4, buy cough medicine, maybe bring her hot soup. But what if I got sick? I longed for sleep. I longed for coffee.

I looked at my watch. How soon would Leanne be up? Maybe she had already given the second bed in her room to someone else. I dressed hastily, my ribbed turtleneck and pressed blue jeans a mockery in this impoverished place, and tiptoed down to the pay phone at the end of the hall.

"Good morning, the Washington Hilton. How may I direct your call?" The receptionist's drawl was smooth silk.

"Yes, Leanne Manning's room please," I whispered.

"You'll have to speak louder, ma'am. Who?"

"I'm sorry. Leanne Manning. She's a guest with you." My voice echoed like a ship's horn down the dark hallway.

When Leanne answered, her voice was muffled with sleep until she heard who was calling. Then it dissolved into laughter. "So, what happened to your great plan to mingle with the granola-eating multitudes? You ended up in a homeless women's shelter? Are you crazy? It's a wonder you didn't get mugged." I tried to imagine the coughing woman knocking me down on her way to the bathroom. Yes, Leanne said, the other bed was empty. "For sweet sake, what do you mean you're not sure? Just get over to the hotel, okay? The march will start soon and I have to take off. But I'll see you afterwards and we can have dinner with my friends. Stop trying to save the world."

Back in my room, I sat for a long time on the bed looking at the grilled windows on an apartment building across the street. A line of laundry hung limply between them. People live here, I thought. How can I tell the lady downstairs I have to leave? Bleeding heart liberal, Leanne said I was. Is that what I am? The room next door was quiet. The woman doesn't need me. What could I have been thinking? She probably has her own cough syrup. Reassured, I zipped my makeup kit and nightgown into the suitcase, folded the blanket neatly at the end of the bed and let myself out.

There was no one downstairs. Should I ring the message bell on the desk? I could leave money next to it and unbolt the front door myself. How much money? I was pulling out my wallet when the door behind the desk opened and the woman, her arms folded over the same misbuttoned sweater, stood leaning against the frame.

"You need somethin'?" She looked at my bag. "You goin' so soon?"

My cheeks warmed. "Well, you see, something has come up. My plans have unexpectedly changed." I dropped my eyes under the woman's steady gaze, my voice brittle as I lied, the way it did when I elaborately thanked a hostess for a boring evening.

"Yeah, things do that, don't they?" she agreed in a flat tone. "Huh. Didn't like the room."

"Oh no, the room was fine, thank you. How much do I owe?" She shrugged and I handed her a twenty and then a five. Was that enough? "Goodbye, thank you again. Umm, is there a bus?" But the woman was already closing the door.

After half an hour, a bus pulled in next to the deli, and it was a relief to ride away, free from the troubles I had left behind. Maybe Leanne is right. I talk big and do nothing. By the time I'd left my bag at the reception desk, I had just time to take a cab to the crowded park where the march began. Leanne was nowhere in sight, but it was exhilarating to lock arms with other marchers. We strode shoulder to shoulder shouting slogans around the White House in a seemingly endless procession down 17th Street, around the Ellipse, up 14th Street and back again.

Women have a right to choose!

Pro Child, Pro Choice!

Fight, Fight! Abortion is a Civil Right!

This is making a difference, I thought. I forgot I was tired, that I'd never had coffee. I forgot about the woman in Room 4. Back at the hotel, the lobby was crowded and I found Leanne waiting for me in a lounge where plants cascaded from the skylight. Talking about the march, we drank chilled chardonnay and consumed a plate of appetizers while a man in a tuxedo played light jazz on a grand piano.

"So, why was it you went to this so-called Y in the first place?" Leanne wanted to know. "What was it like?"

"It wasn't what I thought it would be at all. There was this lady in the room next to mine with a terrible cough. She's there right now by herself." I remembered her thin body. Had she had an abortion? Or maybe there was a child somewhere.

"That's tough," said Leanne. "But I still can't believe you stayed there. Anyway, you're here now." She glanced at her watch. "Can you catch the waiter's eye? We have time for another round before we meet my friends." Warmed by the wine, my unease at being at the hotel began to fade. I signaled to the waiter, stretched out my legs and settled deeper into my chair.

Showers of Blessings

"Hey, Reverend Darryl, How's it going?"

"Hiya, Milk Lady." The pastor of the Church of Showering Blessings in Oakland always greeted me with a hug. Strong, with a friendly reserve, his white teeth, like Harry Belafonte's, flashed under high cheekbones.

"You let me carry that now, I don't want you hurting yourself. You know we count on the Milk Lady." He pulled a blue crate of milk cartons out of the back of my orange van. "You wait there. I'll get the empties."

One Christmas, not long after my Washington trip, I had searched a local newspaper for an organization where I could volunteer, where I could make a difference. I liked the sound of one: the Daily Bread Berkeley Food Project. It sounded easy enough. One day a week, a volunteer picks up extra food or cartons of milk from a restaurant or market and takes them to a needy organization. No hassle, no fuss. A few hours driving and the job is done. I called the woman in charge and was reprimanded in return.

"You want to volunteer at Christmas? Sure. Everyone wants to volunteer at Christmas. If you're serious about wanting to help, you'll call me in January." I'll show her, I thought. In January, filled with self-righteousness, I called her back and was promptly assigned the Oak Haven Market, a small grocery I'd never heard of in the Oakland hills. My job every Friday was to count the coupons customers had donated, exchange them for cartons of milk and drive them to a church on the other side of Oakland.

My friends would say it wasn't "a good neighborhood," but I felt oddly at ease driving down this wasteland of an avenue that stretched into nowhere. The church looked more like a store than a place of worship in the faded building it shared with the Ebony Lady Hair Salon where two hair dryers stood next to empty chairs. Sometimes the proprietor, Delia, was standing in the doorway and I paused to listen to her worry about how to get more customers. Reverend Darryl's truck, "Hauling Fast and Cheap" lettered across its splintering sides, was sometimes parked in front. If he wasn't there, he left the key to the church with Sam who lived upstairs. Sam's window looked across the street to gas pumps where men lounged about in two's and three's or tinkered under rusted hoods.

One Friday of each month, two women cooked a charity lunch in the church meeting hall, and when they saw my van, they called to me through the pungent smell of spattering fish and stale air. "How'r'ya, Honey! Come on in!" I held my breath against the fishy smell as I hauled milk crates past tables set with flowered oilcloth and plastic forks. The over-sized refrigerator was empty except for its vats of hot dog mustard and Kool-Aid on the bottom shelf.

"Come on and sit down here, Baby, and get some lunch. Ain't you hungry?" I liked being called "Baby." No one called me "Baby" where I came from. One woman, vast under her apron, handed me a paper plate wilting under squares of deep-fried fish, French fries and a scoop of coleslaw dripping with milky mayonnaise. Apologetic, I shook my head. I felt embarrassed to sit at the oilcloth table while the women worked so hard, their faces shiny from the heat. And I couldn't imagine eating the unappetizing looking food offered with such pride. When she laid a piece of wax paper across the plate, I put it on the front seat of my van, pretending I would eat it "later on."

Other Fridays, when there was no one at the church, I rang the buzzer next to the gated stairway leading to the upper floor. Sam leaned out the window grinning down at me behind his missing teeth as if I were his best friend. "Hiya, Milk Lady, you wait there, I'll be coming down." Stooped and grizzled, he made his way down dingy carpeted treads one step at a time, fumbled with the lock and squinted into the sidewalk's light. The patterns of veins across the whites of his eyes always reminded me of Proctor who had dug ditchs in our backyard when I was young.

"So, how's it going, Sam?"

"I'm doin' good, Baby, thanks be to the Lord, legs hurtin' some, but I'm doin' pretty good." He rooted around for keys in his stained pants, unlocked the church, and followed me to the van where he grunted with the effort of lifting a loaded crate. "It's okay. Ah got it, Ah got it."

One Friday, I pulled up at the church to find a man, half crouched on the vacant sidewalk as if he'd been waiting for me. He knocked on the door of the van. "Lady, can you give some help?" I slid across the seat to roll down the window. Wide-eyed and gaunt, his yellowish dark skin was dotted with lesions, and his hands shook when he leaned his elbows against the door. Hepatitis, I thought, or maybe AIDS? He must have AIDS.

"What's up?" I tried to sound casual. My job description did not include getting involved with someone this sick.

"Darryl's gone all day." The man stared at the sidewalk. "I need to get to the corner store. I can't hardly walk, Lady, sure do 'preciate you." I remembered Michael's gentleness back in Annie's hospital room. "I volunteer at an AIDS Hospice," he had said. "That's my calling." Michael had been there for us that morning. This man must be a friend of Reverend Darryl's. If I help him, I'll be helping the Reverend too. That's what Michael would have done.

"Yes, of course, get in, I'll give you a ride. What's your name?" He mumbled something I didn't catch as he struggled to open the door. I tried again. "Where do you live?" He pointed at a duplex two doors away.

I waited for him at the corner grocery, and back at the duplex, I carried his grocery bag and pack of sodas behind him to the door. He turned, hunching his shoulders down as if he might fall. "God Bless you, Lady, could you just help me get them up the stairs?" I peered at the dark stairwell with misgivings, but thought of Michael again. He would have gone with the man, and I could too.

We inched our way up into the room where I was repelled by dishes filthy with leftover food spilled across the kitchen counter and one lone cigarette floating in a cup next to the sink. The man hobbled across the carpet to collapse onto a soiled couch and close his eyes. I can't leave the kitchen in such a disgusting mess, I thought, and did what I could with a dented scrub brush, scraping and stacking dishes. It's not much, I thought, but it's something.

"I'm going now," I said to the man on the couch. No response. Well, I thought with pride, I've made a difference. Now I can go home.

The next week, Reverend Darryl met me at the door of the sanctuary. There was no greeting in answer to mine. His face stern, his jaw tight, he was in front of me in one stride, his hands gripping my shoulders. "Don't you ever do that again."

I took a step back, hurt and surprised at his anger. "What? Do what?"

"You went upstairs into a strange man's apartment with no one else around. You have no idea who…"

I interrupted, defensive. "But he seemed so sick. He needed help. "

"You need to know that man has just gotten out of prison for being involved in an attempted murder. He's on serious parole. You don't know what you're messing with, do you hear what I'm saying? Don't go where you don't belong." He turned abruptly, leaving me red-faced and shaken.

For weeks, I avoided the preacher until one Friday he met me at the van. "Hiya, Milk Lady," he greeted me as if he'd forgotten he'd been upset. "Guess you ought to know, Sam's in the hospital. From now on, I'll be here to give you the key." The Reverend's tone was dismissive, but to me a hospital meant a crisis and maybe I could help. As if I were a member of their community, I plunged on.

"Oh, no! I'm so sorry. Poor Sam. Is he going to be all right? What happened?"

Reverend Darryl held up his hand. "Diabetes," he said shortly. "He'll be home next week, so don't worry, okay? He's doing fine."

I reddened. What seemed to me to be friendly concern turned out to be interference in their business. Darryl made it clear that try as I would, we were not friends. It was hard for me to see the line.

The Indignities of Advancing Age

Mother's voice on the phone one afternoon was an octave higher and twice as loud as when she announced other crises. Like the night Wendy, the poodle, met up with a skunk, or the time Mother drove Gladys-the-Buick through the back of the garage. But this time was different. It was Dad.

Now in his mid-eighties, my father had fallen, not because he lost his balance, but because his legs had simply given way beneath him. "And no one knows why. You have to come immediately." Mother's voice was shrill. "I don't know what we're going to do!" Her fear jumped out of the phone at me, and the habitual calm reassurance I always used with Mother kicked in. The yawning hole of everyone's dependency was opening around me again.

The plane made its descent into the Burbank airport, and I leaned my head against the window to watch the familiar San Gabriel mountains rise up behind infinite stretches of Los Angeles houses dozing under a thin blanket of early haze. "Cracker Boxes," Mother called them.

At the hospital, Dad lay patiently, smiling awkwardly at having become the center of attention. "Oh, hello, Dear," he sighed when he saw me at the door. "This is all rather silly don't you think? I'm afraid Mother made you come down, didn't she?"

I kissed him on the forehead. "It's okay, Daddy, I'm overdue for a visit anyway. I'll find out what's going on and we'll figure it out. You're going to be fine." The doctor said it seemed to be a spinal stroke, adding vaguely that physical therapy might help. A nurse said my father had to be catheterized and recommended putting in a supply of diapers. I stared at her with a sudden flash of comprehension. Unable to control his bladder or his bowels, my dignified professorial father had become completely dependent on the women around him, and it had to do with the area of his body that embarrassed him the most. Years later, I would learn that his paralysis had been caused, not by a "spinal stroke," but by an overdose of radiation for an early bout of prostate cancer. Because of my family's timidity about mentioning bodily functions, I had known little about Dad's prostate or that radiation had been involved at all.

He hadn't been home from the hospital more than a few hours before we had our first experience with his private life. "Um, I think there might be signs of some activity down there," he murmured, looking up at me from his wheelchair and gesturing in the direction of his rear. "I think a little investigation might be in order."

"Well, *I'm* not going to do it," said Mother, both anxious and embarrassed. Dad and I looked at each other miserably. I was the only one left.

"Okay, Daddy," I said with a determination I didn't feel. "Let's get you onto your bed and pretend you're in the hospital, and I'm a nurse you'll never see again." This isn't my father, this isn't my father, I repeated silently to myself while I helped him pull down his pajama bottoms and did what I could with a pile of washclothes and a basin of water. It didn't take many of those episodes before I began a search for live-in care.

A white-haired, portly gentleman named James was the first to answer my ad. He must have thought that if he described his previous patients' colons in intimate detail he would get the job; by the end of our interview, I had heard more about his patients' bowels than anyone should know. But he had a kind, comfy face, squinty eyes when he laughed that made him look like a smiling pink marshmallow, and besides, Dad liked him which was good enough for me. "You should know I'm a diabetic," was James's last comment. It didn't matter to me what he was as long as we didn't have to discuss his bowels as well. I sometimes felt surrounded by feces. Every time I took the dog for a walk, Mother would inquire brightly, "Did Wendy do her big one?" I began to have recurrent dreams about overflowing toilets and trying unsuccessfully to clean up bathroom floors.

"Now, James," said Mother in lilting tones. "You're to feel just like a member of the family." James reached out to squeeze her hand and she squeezed and twinkled back.

"And what would you like me to call you?" he asked.

Mother straightened in her chair. "Why, you're to call me Mrs. Lewis," she replied in the regal voice she always used when her Victorian upbringing was back in charge. I hastily ushered James down the kitchen stairs to show him the two rooms that had once been Annie's and mine where Mother and I agreed he could make his apartment. After Annie's death, my father had turned her larger room into an office. On my visits home, I still stayed in the smaller room where I had once read my piles of beauty magazines, examined my pimples in the mirror, and otherwise pined away my early teenage years.

James and I stood together gazing into Dad's office. Seen through his eyes it must have looked shabbily unkempt with its retro painted furniture, a cracked leather chair, and three metal filing cabinets that were not improved by the potted azalea Mother had hastily shoved on top "to give it a homey touch." Annie's collection of ceramic horses had never been moved from its glass case on one wall. "There's even a private entrance through the laundry room," Mother said with satisfaction, oblivious to the mess in the overcrowded space that shared its washing machine and tubs with an ironing board, an antique stove and Dad's tool bench. Standing in the doorway with James, I had to smile at my father's Rube Goldberg heating arrangement: a tiny fan balanced on a zip code directory on top of an old steam radiator that blew heat around the corner of one of the files. Outside the window, the patio, once the scene of congenial parties, lay under a leafy cover of neglect.

James looked at me mournfully. "To think that I have come to this." He drew himself up. "I was a professional man, you know." I tried to ignore a disconcerting wave of apprehension about this fastidious man landing in our household to take care of my vulnerable, rigid, casually informal parents who wanted only to be sitting in the study and left alone.

"How does he like the rooms?" beamed mother from her chair after James had left.

"He said he might do a little decorating," I said hesitantly.

"Well, what's the matter with them?" She looked up from putting a heating pad on her bad knee. "They look perfectly good to me." I didn't yet know what was in store. James moved in, bringing with him, among other things, a TV that took up half the room, filigree decorator lamps, a papier-mâché zebra, gold curlicue mirrors, a cage of finches, a silver tea set, and thirty-six pairs of shoes. "Why on earth does he need thirty-six pairs of shoes?" scoffed Mother who had pretended to be looking for something in James's closet one afternoon when he was gone. "Does he have thirty-six pairs of feet?"

As my mother slowly lost control over her domestic domain, she began to wage subtle warfare with James. Where James was going to eat had been an issue from the beginning, and no amount of mediation on my part could persuade Mother to let him eat with her and Dad. "What would we talk about?" she demanded. On one of my visits, I found her pulling everything she could reach out of the kitchen cupboards. "It's my kitchen, dammit," she was muttering. "He's put everything in the wrong place and not only that, he's telling me we should get a new stove." We both looked at the oven door held tight by a strip of duct tape. "It's a perfectly good stove," she declared and headed for her chair, leaving me to remember the countless casseroles she had cheerfully cooked in that same oven when my Vassar roommates had visited for a glorious month one summer years before.

From his wheelchair, Dad watched these dramas play out with his usual quiet stoicism. "Conflict in general can prove to be unfruitful," he murmured. When he could summon the energy, he pulled himself up on his walker, and with his urine bag dangling, he desperately tried to persuade his legs to regain their former use. I could never persuade James to stop calling him "Hon", or "Babe", and as the months passed, it hurt my heart to see my scholarly father withdrawing into passivity as he lost one dignity after another.

Sometimes Mother persuaded him to join her on the front deck where he stared quietly into space or pretended to listen while she read aloud. I never ceased to marvel at the contrast between my parents' life and the baseball games in the park directly across the street. While they sat behind the wooden gates and sprawling hedge, the park filled with Latino and black families on holidays and weekends, calling to each other and cooking barbecue on outdoor grills. Music from the Good Humor truck mingled with shouts of "Hey, battah, battah, battah! Hey battah!" that cheered on teams of young athletes from all over town.

It was Geneen, James's cousin, who saved my life. James's greatest pleasure was dressing up and driving his capacious Cadillac to Las Vegas for one of the weekends he had off. On one such occasion, James suggested that while he was away, Geneen could take his place. With her sophisticated clothes and sleek blonde hair, she might have been sipping a cocktail in a country club. Instead, blessed by a calm nature and a sense of humor, she listened endlessly to Mother's laments and went about her chores for Dad with quiet patience. Being deeply religious, she would have been the first to say she had been sent by the grace of God.

It was Geneen who was with Dad the night he died. "When he passed, he saw the light of God," she told me later, and though it seemed unlikely, I always hoped she was right.

A doctor wrote "cardiac arrest" on the death certificate, but in the privacy of my heart, I believed my father could simply no longer stand the business of living. I sometimes thought that for him, the challenge of getting out of his life was a scientific problem that could only be solved on his own terms, by quietly slipping away.

Mother believed without a fragment of a doubt that when the Neptune Society sent Dad's ashes in the mail, they weren't actually his. "Can you believe the mailman brought the box to the door like an ordinary package?" she asked me for what seemed like the hundredth time. "How do I know whose ashes those are? They could be *anybody's*!" Her grief was palpable. I had not been there when my father died, and I regularly beat on myself for not having made the arrangements to pick up his ashes from the Neptune Society myself.

For better or worse, after Dad's death, Mother asked James to stay on. I ached for them both, these two lonely people living side by side, not quite as friends, not quite as employer and hired help, but somewhere in between. I labored under the belief that I had to solve every problem, but to my relief, Geneen gradually became a regular along with James. As time passed, I was able to limit the number of trips I made to Altadena and to leave after each visit with an easier frame of mind.

In Berkeley, my camera had increasingly become the focus of my life. I built my own darkroom in the back of what had been Annie's garage, balanced developing pans on the washing machine and hung black curtains across the door. Taking portraits of people could become a form of therapy, I thought, and without looking back, I gave up my psychology studies, and began taking photographs of anyone who would let me near.

A Photograph for Shaquilla

"Why do you want to photograph women here?" Lawanda, a case manager at the Women's Daytime Drop-In Center, asked as she leaned back in her chair with a broad, infectious smile. The office was crowded with boxes spilling over with used clothing.

"I don't know," I said, smiling nervously back. It was my first visit to this agency in Berkeley, known to everyone as the Drop-In, that offered services and hot meals during the day to homeless women and children. I was looking for a place where I could use my camera with the vague idea that I could make a difference by doing something I loved. "I just like to take photographs and maybe I could use my camera to help people," I said. "Maybe the women here would like a nice picture of themselves?" My voice trailed off. "Or maybe they wouldn't."

"Maybe they would, maybe they wouldn't," said Lawanda. "We've never had anyone photographing here."

"I want to make a difference," I said. How lame was that? Lawanda obviously makes a difference every day.

"Well, you'll have to come first as a regular volunteer. We can't have someone just walk in and start taking pictures. You'll have to earn their trust. I know they're needing a cook on Thursdays. What do you say?"

"Okay," I said without enthusiasm. "For a few weeks. Then I'll photograph." I don't want to be a cook, I thought impatiently. I already have a volunteer job driving milk. I want to do something special, something creative of my own. I shifted on the metal chair. Maybe it's just ego, I thought uncomfortably. Maybe I only want to be someone special, to feel as if I were important. Lawanda smiled and said nothing.

Yet I soon found that I liked coming to this ordinary house with its casual little kitchen. The cooking part was easy. I liked filling plates with the kinds of casseroles I'd cooked for my family all my life. But it was harder to know how to talk to the clients, most of whom were black women. I felt awkwardly shy. It wasn't right that I had a nice house and my own car while these women had to walk to shelters, or, if they were lucky, take the bus. Why did I think they'd want someone with a fancy camera to come in and take their photographs? Because they were homeless and poor? Humbled, I stayed in the kitchen and cooked.

One morning, one of the women came in to wash breakfast dishes while I struggled to open a dozen cans of beans with an antiquated can opener. "Take care now you don't cut your hand on those lids," she said. "If you wait a minute, I'll help with that. My name's Brenda." She dried her hands on a towel next to the stove and reached to shake my hand.

"It's good to meet you." I sounded absurdly formal.

"You new?"

"I've only been here a few weeks." Brenda's friendly warmth made me bolder. "Actually, I came to take photographs. If people want them, I mean." I hesitated. "Would it be okay if I took your picture? I have my camera here. If you want, I'll give you a copy when I come next time."

"Why, Honey, I'd be pleased." Brenda beamed. "Wait now 'til I fix my hair." When she was ready, we found morning light on the front porch where she sat looking into the camera without a hint of self-consciousness. As I rotated the lens, Brenda's face popped into focus with a personal intimacy so vivid it made me catch my breath. I was excited; I had never photographed anyone that close. "You are beautiful," I said suddenly. Because it was true.

Later, at home in the darkroom, her face came to life in the developing pan, the contrasts emphasizing the light in her

136

eyes. Her skin shone and an earring glinted from behind her hair. The next week, when I gave her the photograph, she stood looking at it for a long time. "I never had a picture like this," she said, and showed it to another woman. "Look at this. That lady. Look what she gave me." The photograph was passed around.

"It looks real professional," one woman said.

"Will you take my picture?" asked another.

"If I brought my daughter, would you take hers?" asked a third.

Before long, I was taking photographs of anyone who asked. Over time, I photographed babies, families, grandmothers, and a woman in a wheelchair with the saddest face I'd ever seen.

I was fascinated by these women and their lives so different from mine. There was a dignity in their faces, a pride in themselves, and an ease of being that I envied. It was fun to be called the "Picture Lady." The women were proud when I hung their photographs on the living room walls. "Look at me, I'm on the wall," I heard them say. And the more the frames filled with faces, the more my shyness fell away. I was doing something that made a difference. And I belonged.

Using the camera as an introduction, it was easier to talk with the women. We laughed together, and sometimes we hugged. There were stories of evictions I had never known could happen, of domestic abuse, the loss of a partner or a job. One woman showed me a bruise on the side of her face she had hidden beneath a scarf. Another told me proudly about starting back to school. Sometimes when I asked a client how she "was doing," she would answer serenely, "I'm blessed." I didn't see how someone so poor could feel blessed. Wasn't I the one who ought to feel blessed? Was I blessed by God? I didn't know.

I made mistakes. One woman told me how she had to take three buses to the Social Security office in Hayward with her two kids. "So I'm carrying Jamie like the whole way cause he's sick. And when I finally get there, I find out the office is closed."

"That's terrible," I said, reaching to touch her arm. "I know just how you feel." Her eyes narrowed and she stepped back, pushing away my hand.

"No, you don't."

"You're right." My face reddened with embarrassment. "Of course, I don't." How could I?

Some of the women showed signs of mental illness that made me nervous. Embarrassed, I would turn away. But I learned. There was Vinnie. She kept up a steady stream of conversations with her voices that I thought were directed at me. Unable to understand her, I pretended I was busy doing something whenever she headed my way. Then one day I tried a new tact. "Vinnie, would you like a hug?" So abrupt was my question that she stopped in the middle of her river of words and nodded. I had made a friend.

When Lawanda had time, she liked to hang out in the kitchen to joke about her diets and how much she ate. One day, she leaned her comfortable body against the doorframe, her face sober. "Do you remember photographing a woman named Shaquilla?"

I tried to remember. It bothered me that I found many black women's names confusing. I could remember names like Susan or Sarah, but unfamiliar syllables seemed to float away. "Shanika?"

"No. Shaquilla. She was here off and on for a while. Maybe not on the days you're here."

"I can't place her. Is her picture in the living room?"

"I didn't see it. I looked for it after her brother called me yesterday. He told me Shaquilla passed last weekend."

"Passed? She died? I'm so sorry. Was she sick?"

"I don't know for sure." Lawanda lowered her voice. "Her brother didn't say, but I know she had a drug problem. Anyway, some of us are going to a service this coming Friday. I thought maybe you'd like to come along." I was flattered to be asked. It made me feel important to be treated like one of the staff.

That Friday, four of us drove with Lawanda past hopeless looking strip malls and gritty houses that reminded me of Reverend Darryl's church. We parked in front of a storefront with Haven Baptist Church spelled out above the door. Inside, it was cool and immaculately white with six rows of pews and a sprinkling of mourners. A cross hung behind a wooden platform that held Shaquilla's simple coffin, and I was relieved to see that it was closed. Two lanky men with wrists sticking out of Sunday suits stood in front of a bouquet of pink and white gladiolas. One of them waved at Lawanda, who went to speak with them while the other women and I took a seat in a back pew. An organ wheezed, and when the men joined the family sitting up front, I was elated to see an enlarged photograph glued into a cardboard frame and leaning against the gladiola vase.

I caught my breath. "That's my photograph," I said out loud and stood to get a better look. Now I remembered Shaquilla, a sullen-looking client, who had turned away when I'd asked if she would like me to take her photograph.

"I don't want no picture," she had muttered. "I got no teeth."

"It doesn't matter. If you change your mind, let me know. I'm here every Thursday." To my surprise, the next week she had changed her mind. Later, I took special care in my darkroom and was proud of the way it turned out. Her thin face was turned slightly to show a grave rather than sulking expression and there was no sign of toothless gums. But when I gave it to her the next week, she only glanced at it.

"I look terrible. I don't want it on the wall," she grumbled and, snatching it out of my hand, stuck the picture in her bag. I was stung by her lack of appreciation of my work.

"I never put a photo on the wall if you ask me not to," I said in an injured tone. "But I think you look really nice." So much for that, I thought. I never should have bothered. The woman left after lunch, and I hadn't seen her again. When Lawanda slid into the pew next to me, I squeezed her arm. "Lawanda, look up there! Leaning against the flowers. Shaquilla's photograph. I took that."

"I know," Lawanda whispered. "Her brother told me it was the only photograph of Shaquilla the family had."

A minister came in from a side door and took his place in front of the coffin. "Brothers and Sisters, beloved family," he intoned. "We have come here today to celebrate our dearly departed Sister, Shaquilla." I looked at her photograph again. My dad would have been proud of me, I thought, and remembering him and our times together in his darkroom, my eyes burned from holding back the tears.

Jayda

The next week, I met Jayda. In the Drop-In's overstuffed living room, there was a flurry of women talking, with Lawanda's laugh wafting above the others. From the kitchen doorway, I could see a large woman standing in the open front door, smiling awkwardly at the attention. She was tall, a solid bear of a woman, with a backwards baseball hat covering close-cropped hair. A tie-dye T-shirt hung over athletic pants.

Lawanda wrapped the woman in her arms. "Whazzup, Girl? I didn't think you'd come." Other women who seemed to know this newcomer waited their turn to hug her before Lawanda led her to the kitchen. "This here's Jayda," she said to me. "She's been my best friend since I can remember." I held out my hand, but instead, Jayda pulled me into an embrace, her ample breasts pressed above mine.

"I'm a hugger," she said. Her voice was round.

"How's it going?" I mumbled, my mouth flattened against her shirt. Jayda probably hugged everyone like that, but during the rest of my shift, I felt her eyes on me, and when I smiled at her, her dimples deepened when she smiled back.

Lawanda told me later that Jayda was on disability and struggled with depression. "She went to one of those trade schools, got a good job doing sheet metal work. But then she fell off the scaffolding, dropped a whole story and landed on her feet. It threw out her back. I think she was pushed." I tried to imagine that big body balanced on a scaffold. "When she went on disability, she got real down," Lawanda was saying. "I mean I was scared for her. You hear what I'm saying? So I got her to come to the Drop-In."

"Why do you think she was pushed?"

"Hey. She's a black woman, right? And a lesbian? Doing guys' work?"

Lesbian. My exposure to gay women had been limited to a time when my mother mentioned, with some discomfort, that two women down the street were probably "some of those homo people." At Vassar, I never thought about whether any of my classmates were lesbians. Where was I all that time? I didn't know. Like most people, I had read about the AIDS crisis and visited the Quilt when it was on display, but the gay-lesbian struggle had remained peripheral to my world.

Each week, I looked forward to finding Jayda settled at one of the Drop-In's dining room tables with their brightly checked tablecloths and vases of flowers that had seen better days. She was always joking with Lawanda and talking with the women who came by. She didn't look depressed now that Lawanda had asked her to be a volunteer at the Drop-In instead of a client. I was pleased that her volunteer shift was going to be on Thursdays, the same day as mine. I liked the way she listened, hugging whoever might be close, and when she tilted back her chin to laugh, she made everyone around her laugh too. She made it easy for me to join in, to chatter and joke with them even if sometimes I didn't quite get what was funny.

Once when I came in from photographing a woman outside, Jayda pointed at my camera. "Hey, Picture Lady, when are you going to take my photograph?"

"Now if you like." Suddenly apprehensive, I expected her to laugh into the camera, but alone in my darkroom, her image stared back at me, ageless, androgynous and questioning. Why am I so drawn to you, I asked myself, you who are twenty-five years younger than me and from another world? I wanted to give her the photograph right away, but she didn't show up at the Drop-In the next Thursday or the Thursday after that. The third week, she was still gone, but there was a poem pinned to the living room wall.

My Sister, My Sister
I see your tears falling
To your ankles with the rest of your cares
Like falling stars
Wasting on cold cement.

Above the poem, she had drawn a child-like picture of a blonde angel in a white dress with a halo and wings. And underneath,

"Dedicated to the women here who saved my life.
You are all my angles [sic]. Jayda."

The following week, she was back. I wanted to sound cool, like Lawanda. "Hey, Girl. Where you been?" But she only shrugged. "I wanted to tell you," I started, "The poem you wrote is what my photos are about."

"Of course," she said with another shrug, as if she thought I wasn't very smart.

Weeks later at one of the Drop-In's volunteer meetings, Lawanda asked me to bring in a few of the photos I had enlarged. When I spread them out on the worn blue carpet, everyone hitched forward to look at the faces who looked calmly back while I filled the silence with nervous chatter. "Well, of course, standing alone the photos don't mean anything, I mean, I was thinking they need something else, but maybe if I…" Behind me, Jayda interrupted.

"I can write poetry for them." I turned to look at her. Her eyes held mine, her expression intense. "I can look at their faces and tell their truth." Yes, I thought, I think you can. I looked away, unexpectedly flustered.

Women around us were nodding, and one woman, a board member wearing a business suit, spoke up. "If you framed your photos together with Jayda's poems, you would have a photography show. You could put them up in my office where I

143

often have exhibits. We could have a reception and publicize the Drop-In at the same time." Before I could think of an answer, everyone was talking and agreeing on a date. I was excited. I'd always wanted a real gallery show.

But the next week Jayda had disappeared again. Where had she gone this time? When's she going to write the poems? Nervousness was creeping in and I felt shy to call her. One morning, while I cooked a pot of spaghetti in the crowded kitchen, an angular black woman appeared in the doorway, shifting back and forth and grinning at me. "Hey, you the Picture Lady? I'm a friend of Jayda's. My name's Tina, even if I'm not tiny." She let out a high-pitched laugh at her own joke that made me feel uneasy. "Jayda said to ask you, could I bring some photographs to her and she'd write stuff for 'em and I'll bring 'em back."

"But where is she? Is something wrong?"

"Nahh, Jayda's okay, she's just in the hospital for a while. She's depressed. You know what I mean?"

I didn't know what she meant. A mental hospital? Was that where Jayda was? Could I trust Tina? What had I gotten myself into? Reluctantly, I gave her four of the photographs in a manilla envelope. But true to her word, the next week she was back, grinning and weaving, with the photos and some penciled poetry on sheets of paper torn from a composition book. Some poems were childlike, written without much thought; others showed a wisdom that could only come from the streets. Jayda had been right. Each poem, in its own way, told a truth. More envelopes of photographs went back with Tina, and when she brought them back, I typed the poems out and framed them together with the photographs. But still no word from Jayda.

Three days before the show, my kitchen phone rang and there was Jayda. "Oh, thank God." My voice was a shout. "Are you all right?"

"I'm fine. Don't worry, it's all good."

"But you do know we're putting on an exhibit with a reception this Friday? You're not going to disappear again, are you?"

"That's why I'm calling. What kind of shoes should I wear?"

"Shoes? Good grief, Jayda, it doesn't matter what kind of shoes you wear. Any kind of shoes. Just show up, okay?"

The night of the reception, I smiled at guests who chatted together while they drank wine. The crowded gallery space was warm with light, but my hands were cold with nervousness. My photographs and Jayda's poems were on display for everyone to criticize. Would she show up? She said she wanted to bring her family, but how would they feel about being there? If they came at all. I tried not to watch the door.

But then she was there, wearing her new brown shoes and looking cool-headed as could be with her family crowded behind her. Her expressionless mother called me "ma'am" and went to sit on a straight-backed chair in a corner. There were two sisters, both as large as Jayda, and a pair of handsome young men who looked like her. "These are my twin brothers, Jacob and John. They're getting ready to go in the army."

"Pleased to meet you," they said in unison, and went to stand next to Jayda's mother like the National Guard. The gallery hostess dinged a spoon against a wine glass and made a short welcoming speech before she turned unexpectedly to Jayda.

"Would you read some of your poetry for us?" For the first time, Jayda seemed caught off guard. I had expected her to jump at the chance to read, but she looked shyly at her shoes and shook her head. She poked her younger sister, Patricia.

"You read."

"Do I have to?" Patricia looked at me, laughing nervously.

"You can do it, Patricia," I said, nudging her towards a photo of a weary looking mother with two children peeking out from behind. Patricia took a breath and began speaking in a full, expressive voice. The faces in the photograph came alive.

We must be ghosts, or maybe someone's nightmare.
People pass us by like they don't see us, not even the kids.

We must be ghosts
Or maybe someone's nightmare
They take wide steps quickly so
No one can hear the tears
That gather on the ground.

When my children ask
Why people don't seem to care
How can I say
We must be ghosts or maybe someone's nightmare?

The room was quiet. "Read another," someone said. Warming to the attention, Patricia read a second poem under a photograph of two laughing children.

My spirit soars with eagles
My laugh makes angels smile
My tears make flowers bloom
My voice makes buildings shake
My hands? Well, they tell lullabyes.

And then a third, all to applause. "You could make this into a performance piece," whispered a friend standing next to me.

"Yes," I said. "I suppose we could." But I couldn't imagine how.

Soul Connection

After the gallery show and in between trips to 596 to sooth James, comfort Mother, and listen to Geneen, Jayda and I met regularly at a library near the Drop-In. Heads bent, we edited her poetry and matched it with new photos. I liked the nearness of her body and the gentle way she read.

One rainy afternoon, she was reading from a new poem:

Who was I supposed to be?
Half my childhood is missing from my mind.
Maybe the abuse, the drugs, the rapes
Were to get me ready for my victim role.

Who was I supposed to be?
Who have I become? ...

I stopped her. "Your poetry. It's about you, isn't it?"

"You don't want to know."

Actually, I did want to know. "Only if you want to tell me." We both stared out the window where rain made patterns against the glass. She examined her fists, nails bitten to the quick.

"When I was little, maybe five, I liked to skip along the sidewalk. I could hear the bees and smell the flowers. But one time, an old man in a doorway said if I came into his house, he'd give me some candy. I didn't get candy much so I went. Inside it smelled real bad. He said if I touched him he'd give me some more." When she did look at me, her face was empty. "Then he unzipped himself and made me...You know. He said he'd tell my dad what I'd done if I didn't come back. So I did. It was like I was dead."

"Jayda, you don't have to talk about this stuff, you know."

"I want to talk about it 'cause you listen. When I was thirteen, I was raped by my…" She stopped. "I don't want to talk about who did it. Someone in my family. But after that, I got fatter. I didn't know I was pregnant or nothin'. My mom never talked about it. Then I got a terrible stomach ache. They were so mean to me at the hospital. I yelled at them and they gave me a shot, and when I woke up my body felt like it was broke in half. They told me I had two babies, but I was too young and they took them away."

"Thirteen," I murmured, trying to understand how such a horrific experience could be real. When I was thirteen, I was off pretending I was a cowboy on my horse. Two white women sat down at a table on the far side of the room, and I looked at them as if they could give me some reassurance that the kind of abusive tragedy Jayda was describing hadn't really happened, as if the world I was used to was still there.

Her voice dropped to a whisper. "My mom and dad told everyone those babies were theirs, and raised them like their own. I ran away, lived in foster homes and in Golden Gate Park under a bridge with some homeless folks. But they were good to me and got me to go to school. My teacher, Miss Lane, she helped me write." Jayda kept talking as if she couldn't stop. "When I went home I had to pretend the twins were my brothers. My father, he said everything was my fault. He used to be a boxer. It's hard to believe because he's so sick now, has to use oxygen, but he used to beat me with a leather belt." She gave a short laugh. "When I was older I learned how to take him down in a head lock. He didn't touch me after that."

I sat for a long time, trying to imagine what it must have been like for her, what I could do to help. "The twins," I said, slowly. "John and Jacob that I met at the gallery. They're your own boys."

Jayda nodded. "They don't know I'm their real mom. They think I'm their sister."

After that afternoon, we talked often on the phone in the evenings, our conversation straying to other parts of our lives. I liked the way she listened as if she cared. When I told her more about myself, about my family and my marriage, she said it was important.

"You know," she said, "We're both survivors." Me? I had never thought of myself as a survivor. As privileged, maybe, or lucky, or both. But not a survivor. Her voice was quiet and insistent inside the phone. "We got soul connection. You know that, don't you? It's like we knew each other in another life." I hesitated. How could I have soul connection with a woman so unlike anyone I had ever known? But I could feel it too. Maybe she was right.

The Readers

"You could make this into a performance," my friend had said that night at the gallery. I knew the photographs were good, and enlarged on a screen they would be powerful. And Patricia's voice had brought them to life. I was excited. "I could make the photographs into slides," I said to Jayda, "And project them really big on the wall. And two readers' voices could bring your words out of the dark as if the poetry were coming from the photographs themselves. We could have a script, and you and your sister could read the poems. We could tell a story about women and homelessness. What do you think?"

"There's no way I'm going to read," Jayda said flatly. "I'll read to you, but I'm not reading from a script to no audience. If you can talk Patricia into it, okay. But you can't rely on her to show up. Let's get more readers than just her."

Patricia seemed reliable enough, but we ended up with three more women to read in addition to Patricia, all of them friends of Jayda's. There was Tina, the woman at the Drop-In with the edgy laugh. There was Lawanda's girlfriend, Mona, who said she was an actress. And finally, Jayda wanted to ask Brittany, the girlfriend of her son John, one of the twins.

The day of our first rehearsal at Jayda's older sister's house in Vallejo, I was careful to arrive at exactly four o'clock. I sat on the front porch to wait. More than a half hour passed before Jayda sauntered up the path, a six pack of sodas in one hand and a bag of chips in the other. She didn't notice when I made a big show of looking at my watch, and neither did Patricia, who wasn't far behind. "I'm not going to read," Patricia pouted when she saw me. "I'm not good enough. And besides," she glowered at her sister, "Jayda's too bossy." I began to feel uneasy about what I thought would be a simple rehearsal.

Mona came in next, with her close-cropped hair dyed a white blonde and hoop earrings the size of teacups. I wondered how anyone could walk in shoes like that as she balanced into the living room on three-inch wedge sandals. "I'm an actress," she announced, examining long crimson nails that matched her lips. I was asking her where she had performed when the screen door slammed and there was Tina. Tinted contacts gave her eyes a green glow.

"I'm an actress too," she interrupted, not to be outdone by Mona. Brittany was last, giggling and hanging on to stoic-looking John while she dabbed at a thin trickle of blood down her calf from a freshly needled tattoo. I stared at her and her bleeding tattoo. This girl couldn't be more than seventeen, I thought, much too young. What are we doing? What am I doing? I didn't know anything about directing theater, especially with a group as different as this one. How could we ever pull this off?

Everyone was laughing at a story Tina was telling, rocking back and forth in time to her words. She was very funny and I found myself laughing with them. I liked the women's easy hilarity and openness with each other, and I wanted them to like me back. When I told John he could be in charge of the music, he smiled for the first time. He helped me balance the projector on one end of a coffee table while the readers went out to smoke, and when I focused the first slide of a somber older woman on the wall, her face commanded the room.

"Girl? You're all right!" I jumped at Tina's voice behind me.

"Girl? So are you," I answered back, flattered by her approval. The other readers drifted in, I handed out the scripts, and was relieved that Patricia forgot she wasn't going to read, and performed the first poem with real feeling. When it was Mona's turn, her diction was sharp, just as she had promised. Maybe this was going to work after all. It was validating to be working with these women, to be living my liberal values instead of just talking about them. But when it was Brittany's turn, her lifeless monotone sounded nothing like the searching face of the young teenager projected on the wall.

Excuse me, sir, have you seen my father?
I know he looks like me
I don't care if he doesn't have a job
Or if he never loved my mother...

After she had read the same lines with the same flat voice for the fourth time, Jayda stood up. "That's it," she said abruptly. "We gotta get a new reader."

"That's typical of you, Jayda," yelled Patricia from across the room. "You're always telling people off."

"Why don't you all shut up," said Tina.

"Calm down," I said, anxiety gripping me. "No one has to leave." I tried to sound firm over my nervousness, to take charge. "Come on, you guys, this is a professional rehearsal. Brittany can learn to read." But Jayda would have none of it. I watched in dismay as she huffed out to the porch to smoke again and Patricia disappeared out the back.

"How can we ever do a show when everyone's angry all the time?" I asked Jayda when she came back, smelling of tobacco. "I hate it when people get so mad."

"Don't you worry, Swee' Pea, it's going to be fine," she soothed. "We all get mad sometimes. Brittany's okay, and Patricia and me, we always fight. It doesn't mean we don't love each other." I remembered a volunteer at the Drop-In who could occasionally come out with a racially tinged comment as if she couldn't hear herself speak. Jayda never failed to wrap her in a hug. "Why do you hug people like Sue Ann who make those barbs?" I had asked.

"Easy. They're the ones who need the hugs the most. It's all about love, Girl. It's all about love."

Her arms went around me. "Dance with me," she whispered in my ear, and for a moment I leaned against the warmth of her bulk.

There was no way we were ready for our first show. We had been invited to perform at a small university in Oakland where a friend of mine taught photography. Our final rehearsal was a disaster. Tina was alternately exuberantly helpful to me or furious with Mona who had said something derogatory about Tina's teenage daughter I couldn't hear. Jayda was mad at Patricia, who sat with her face turned to the wall. Brittany was the only one who paid attention to the script, and John, who was supposed to be running the music, kept falling asleep. "Too much pot," said Jayda succinctly.

Tina decided to spend the rest break counting the number of parts she'd been given, and came up short. "Hey, this isn't fair." Her eyes bugged behind her glasses. "Mona's got more pieces than me. You gave her two of mine and that's not fair. I'm outta this fucking place." She threw her script onto a chair and slammed out the door.

"Good riddance," said Jayda.

"What do you mean, good riddance?" I yelped. "We've got a show to perform next weekend. Someone else will have to learn her part and there isn't time."

"Well, *I'm* not going to read it," snapped Mona on her way out the door.

All week I agonized. Maybe I could persuade Jayda to read Tina's part. What if the rest of the readers decided not to come? Were we going to make fools of ourselves in front of an audience? What if there was no audience? But to my amazement, the afternoon of the performance, the readers arrived adorned in their Sunday best, with Brittany's décolletage nearly falling out of her dress. Tina appeared in a new Raiders sweatshirt to be accepted back by the group as if she'd never left, and an audience made up mainly of my loyal white friends drifted in to perch on folding chairs and stare at the borrowed screen. Finally, every seat was taken. At the prospect of a real audience, the readers, looking scared out of their shoes, huddled in one corner with their backs to the room, whispering among themselves.

"Ladies, we're ready to start," I hissed in my tightest school ma'am voice to their four backs. No response. "Come on, you guys," I cajoled. "Please, you can't read to an audience like that. Everyone's waiting." Then Jayda was there, looming and growling a threat I couldn't hear. Whatever she said worked because the readers turned to straggle into a line next to the screen. "Please, God," I whispered to myself, and projected the first slide, vivid even in a room that was too light. Patricia began on cue, her rich voice filling the room, and when the others read, they sounded nothing like the last rehearsal. Mona was convincingly tender as a young woman holding her aging mother close.

She could be anyone's mother, but she's mine.
Her strength is as deep as the lines carved into her face...

Tina was perfect as a furiously scowling woman.

Dammit, dammit, dammit!
Someone has stolen my life.
I said, someone has stolen my life...

John managed to time the music to the slides, and when the large eyes of a blonde child looked down from the screen, Brittany sounded exactly like the little girl.

I'm so tired.
Can you believe I'm only two...

Sometimes they left out a line or missed a word, and once Tina dropped her script, but to me, they were miraculous.

It was over. The room was silent. They don't like it, I thought. I stared at my lap and tried to remember to breathe. Then, I heard the audience begin to clap. The applause grew louder, and when I looked up, everyone in the room was standing. Jayda was grinning at me. I wanted to hug her, to tell her she was gorgeous, but instead we made our way to the front of the room and gestured towards the line of readers. "Bravo!" someone said. The readers shifted and squirmed, not knowing where to look. To me, they were beautiful. I was in love with them all, and told them so, including Jayda. We're going to make this happen, I thought. Whatever it is we're doing, it's going to work.

A Member of a Family

But the work would have to wait. Jayda's father died. Her voice on the phone, muffled in misery, strengthened to outrage, and ended with a whine of self-pity. "Mom's shut in her room. My sisters won't stop their sobbing. I'm the only one in this whole stupid family who has a driver's license, and I'm sick. I got terrible vertigo and I can't drive and there's no one to pick up Auntie Estie." Except that Jayda's father had been in the army and had been a boxer, all I knew about him were the stories she had told me of his abuse, not only of her, but others in the family. How could the family mourn an abuser? "It doesn't matter about abuse," Jayda had said. "In our family, the wagons circle round no matter what. That's what families do for each other. We take care of our own."

Finally, it became clear that Jayda's Aunt Esther was arriving at the Oakland Airport from Kansas City that afternoon and there was no one to "fetch her to Vallejo for the funeral." You don't need to get involved here, I said to myself. But poor Jayda, I thought, isn't it the least I can do for her after all she's been through? "It's okay," I heard myself saying in my habitually reassuring tone. "I can easily run down and pick up your aunt." At the airport, I thought, I'll just hold up a sign with Esther's name, drive her to Vallejo, and then go home. Quick and easy.

That afternoon at the gate, I stood with my sign in front of passengers straggling in from Kansas City. No Aunt Esther. Did I have the wrong flight? Did she miss her plane? I was about to give up, when a black woman with a stern jaw, upright and spare in a green striped dress, strode through the gate and passed me as if she were on an urgent mission to somewhere else. A cloth bag with double handles banged against her legs. "Wait a minute," I called, waving my sign. "Wait! Esther! I'm here to give you a ride." She threw me one backwards glance and increased her pace. Maybe I have the wrong person, I thought. By now we were jogging towards the revolving door to the street, but to my relief, Esther stopped just short of the door. Out of breath, I darted around in front of her. "Jayda's family asked me to take you to Vallejo," I panted. Who must she think I am? One look and it's obvious I'm not part of the Jackson family. If a strange woman were trying to give me a ride, wouldn't I feel threatened too? But finally, she made a slight motion with her chin that I took to be a nod.

"You can put your bag in the back," I offered, when we finally reached the car hidden somewhere in a sea of glittering windshields. She only clutched it tighter to her chest. Climbing into the passenger seat, she shoved it onto the floor in front of her and sat staring stonily ahead. "Uhhh, seatbelts," I said loudly as I pulled out mine, exaggerating the motion while I snapped it around my chest. I glanced sideways at Esther who sat, immobile as a mummy. I didn't want to reach over her for fear she'd think I was trying to hug her. Finally, she looked at my seatbelt and reluctantly pulled hers across her chest. I held my breath while she fumbled for the clip. It snapped closed.

Safely on the freeway, I attempted conversation. "Is this your first trip to California?"

"Yes, Ma'am."

"Have you lived in Kansas City all your life?"

"Yes, Ma'am."

We rode the rest of the way in an uncomfortable silence until at last we pulled up to the curb outside the family's two-story house. Jayda's three sisters were waving from the porch, and Esther and her bag shot out of the car like a cannonball into their arms and into the house. When I followed her up the steps, I could hear Jayda's oldest sister laughing. "Auntie Estie, you gotta be trippin'. Mer wasn't gonna steal you." Now's my chance to leave, I thought, but before I could get to the car, the sisters had pulled me through the screen door into the shadowed living room filled with plastic-covered furniture. A giant-size photograph of the father feinting a punch in a boxing ring looked down from the wall. Jayda was nowhere in sight.

"Mer, honey," said the sister, "Auntie Estie got something to say." Esther stood grinning sheepishly.

"I'm sure sorry I didn't talk to you, it was just all so new," and she gave me a clumsy, long-armed embrace. Later, at the funeral, I was proud to hear her telling everyone I was her best friend.

Jayda wanted me to sit up front with the family, but the funeral was open casket, and I chose to sit in the back. "You're a member of the family," she whispered.

"No, I'm not!" I whispered back.

When the service was over, the twins, their faces contorted with grief, helped slide the flag-covered coffin into a small hearse parked in front of the church. I was pulling out the keys to my car when Jayda caught up with me on the steps. "We got a problem," she said. "There's another service for families at the military cemetery down near Gustine. Dad's going to be buried there 'cause he was in the army and Mama says we gotta go. There's a ceremony at three o'clock. I'm way too dizzy to drive." I stared at her. Did she think I was going too? I looked around for Lawanda who had been sitting up front next to Jayda.

"Can't Lawanda drive?"

"There's too many of us. We got to take two cars."

The hearse driver's pale face was flushed pink under his chauffeur's cap. "How we gonna get there in time if you people don't hurry up?" he shouted.

"Listen to that guy. *You people* he says," muttered Jayda.

"Where's Gustine?" I asked.

"Not far. Down Route 5. On the way to Fresno." Then I remembered that our faithful, hard-working Gussie had been

159

buried in Gustine. "I don't like it that she's gone so far," the sister had said that afternoon so long ago when I went to visit Mr. Preston with Rosie and Liz.

"Not far! Jayda! There's no way you can make it to Gustine by three." But before I had figured out how to say no, I found myself in the driver's seat of a van filled with Jayda's family: three sisters, the twins, the girlfriend Brittany, and Jayda next to me. We took up the rear behind Lawanda, who was driving Jayda's mother, her oxygen tank, and Auntie Estie. The hearse and its coffin peeled away from the curb to lead the procession at such speed that by the time we were safely on the freeway, my speedometer was close to eighty. In the back of the van, someone turned on some rap music, the main words of which were fuck, bitch and nigga. Younger sister Patricia let out frequent sobs of "Oh, my poor daddy, I can't live without him," while Jayda turned round to glare at her and mutter, "Drama queen." Sodas and bags of potato chips made the rounds.

I could barely keep up with Lawanda and the hearse. "All I need is a chauffeur's hat," I joked, glancing in the rearview mirror at the brown faces in the seats behind.

"Driving Miss Daisy," agreed Jayda, taking a long pull from a cigarette that she stuck out the window in deference to me. Outside the car, wide sprinklers cascaded rainbows of spray across alfalfa fields, and except for the rap music and an occasional keening sigh from Patricia, a kind of peace settled throughout the van. The speedometer hovered at eighty-five mph.

"This is ridiculous," I said. "There's no way we can keep up this speed." Ahead of us, Lawanda must have thought so too because she blasted her horn at the hearse and stuck her arm out the window with a determined flourish of her middle finger. To my surprise, he eased onto the shoulder of the highway and we pulled in behind. Lawanda was out in a flash, puffing her way through soft dirt towards the hearse where she banged on the driver's closed window, waved her arms and yelled some more. When, out of expletives, she turned back to the car, the driver leaned out and flipped her off, a gesture she fortunately missed. Even Patricia joined in the laughter, and our caravan began again at a slower pace until we reached the exit marked Gustine.

At the cemetery gate, the hearse driver said something to the military guard, the gate swung open, and our procession proceeded slowly past large American flags snapping in the valley wind. But beyond the flags, there were no rolling hills of white crosses like the pictures I'd seen of Arlington Cemetery. There were only asphalt roads and a desolate expanse of tired grass divided into lettered subdivisions. It made me sad to think of Gussie buried somewhere in this place, too far for her family to visit. At Area G, an officer in a military car waited for us, and in the field across the road, one soldier sat in a truck with a hoist next to two men digging a grave.

From the van, we watched the hearse drive out to meet the truck. Jayda let out a grunt of disgust and hauled herself out of the passenger seat to confer with the officer. She came round to lean against my open window, the low sun reflecting off the frame of her dark glasses. "The ceremony was an hour ago. The other families have left. That official guy says we can walk out to the hearse where they're digging the grave. If you want to come, we'll have to walk, no cars allowed." Stretching and lighting cigarettes, the sisters helped their mother out of the other car, where she and her oxygen tank leaned against the fender, her face the color of dry cement.

"You guys crazy?" Jayda snapped. "Get those cigarettes away from here. You want to blow up Mama?" Brittany let out a shrill giggle, and I couldn't hide my laughter at the absurdity of her question in this desolate place.

"There's no way we're going to walk way out there and leave poor Mama behind," said Patricia, her arm around her mother.

"It's not right for me to go out there with you," I said to Jayda, feeling awkward in the midst of this family. But as Jayda threaded her way unsteadily through clumps of grass to the hearse, she looked so alone I wished I had gone. The soldier retrieved the flag off the coffin, folded it military style and handed it to Jayda before the truck's crane swung round to pick up the coffin and waft it gently into the waiting grave. Lawanda nudged me. "That man flew through the air like the angel Gabriel himself," she whispered.

Dry-eyed, Jayda handed the flag to her mother as the hearse disappeared down the road without so much as a farewell toot. The rest of us climbed back into our cars and sat for a long moment, alone with our own thoughts. "Poor Daddy, out there all alone," whimpered Patricia while Lawanda started the car ahead of us and I turned the key in the van. The flags now hung limply on their poles as we drove slowly to the guardhouse where the soldier saluted as we passed.

"Backatcha," said Jayda, saluting smartly in return, and everybody laughed. Brittany started the music and Jayda turned to grin at me as if we were returning from a trip to an amusement park instead of burying her father. "Aren't you glad you came?" she asked. I felt her hand slide behind my back, warm and strong. And comforting.

I looked in the mirror at the family in the seats behind. I thought about the tears, the laughter, the good natured acceptance of me into their midst. I had never met a family like this.

"Yes." I smiled. "Yes, I am."

I Got My Baby Back

The funeral was over, and Jayda and I could turn our attention back to producing Sisters performances. There was a rhythm to our work, schlepping, talking, planning what to change, when to rehearse, and how and where to add music. The readers teased us, saying we were in love, and it was true that I could feel myself being pulled in by the strength of Jayda's presence as if we were moving together in a dance. Although rehearsals remained chaotic, during performances, the readers always managed to pull it off. Sometimes, listening to them dramatize Jayda's poetry in harmony with my vivid projections of women and children's faces, the beauty of what we were doing together brought me close to tears.

One such show was at a church in North Berkeley. Jayda finished up our opening talk with a fluorish. "And now without further ado," as if we were the Ringling Brothers, and I started the projector. Half way through the script, the readers started their rhythmic chant,

In your shoes I walk
In your shoes I walk
Sistah! I walk in your shoes
In your shoes
In the morning I dress and put on your shoes, Sistah
I step into the street and
Deal with the world in your shoes
In your shoes...

Suddenly there was a voice from the back of the room. "That's me," said the voice. "That picture is of me." The readers stopped. The audience craned to look.

"Who is that?" I mouthed at Jayda, but she only shook her head. Is the woman coming up the aisle a client? Had I forgotten to get her permission to use the photo? Is she mad at us? But when she was closer, I recognized her as Tanya, a young client I had photographed the year before. She had told me she had gotten pregnant while she was addicted to drugs, and Child Protective Services had taken the baby away to foster care. I remembered her saying resolutely, "I'm going to get myself into a rehab program. I'm going to get my baby back." I was relieved to see that she was smiling, and when she held out her arms, I stepped down from the low stage to meet her.

"Lawanda brought me," she said in my ear. "She wanted me to see my picture up on the screen." I forgot we were in the middle of the script and everyone was waiting. On impulse, I pulled her onto the stage to stand in the light of her photograph.

"This is Tanya," I said.

Tanya smiled some more and spoke to the room without a hint of shyness. "I'm clean," she said. "I'm clean, and I got myself a job, and I got my baby back." The audience was on its feet. The readers finished the poem.

> *I smile at strangers who don't meet*
> *My eyes, and when I cry*
> *My tears fall on your shoes, Sistah.*
>
> *When the day is done I return home and*
> *Begin to remove your shoes, Sistah.*
> *I take off each pair of*
> *Flats, pumps, tennis shoes, work boots,*
> *Sandals and slippers,*
> *And I rub my feet and go to sleep*
> *And I see you in my shoes, Sistah.*

The next week, out of the blue, we received a windfall and everything changed. Two generous checks arrived; one from a man in a suit and tie who had seen the Tanya show and told us he worked for a dot-com; the other from a spinster lady from the Berkeley church who said she had been "profoundly moved." Now there was enough money to buy a used shiny Windstar van, to invest in professional sound equipment, and to give stipends to the readers. The project grew. Gradually, we added new pieces, three more readers, and an engagingly hip ASL interpreter. We were now a troop of nine, too big for the Drop-In to cover our liability and van insurance.

"It is time for the Sisters Project to become a non-profit," urged four loyal friends who agreed to serve on a Board. Reluctantly, I found a lawyer, signed papers, and registered the Sisters Project in Sacramento as an official 501-C3. I was now, I discovered, the Executive Director of a Corporation, a title that would have seemed comical if it hadn't been so daunting. Scared of making a mistake, I was stiff with nervousness at Board meetings as I struggled to learn how to write a grant and to balance even a basic budget with terms like fixed assets and accumulated depreciation. I hired an accountant who, I soon discovered, was as anxious about making a mistake as I was. This was not what I had signed up for, but like a bride who couldn't call off the wedding after the invitations had been sent, I plunged on.

Berkeley High

"The Sisters Project Puts a Face on Homelessness" read a headline in an article in the Chronicle's Datebook section. We were thrilled when it went on to say, "The haunting multimedia show has riveted audiences," but we barely noticed that praise was beginning to muddle our heads. Instead of focusing on our message about women and homelessness, we let our egos take over. Driving back from a program at Stanford, Patricia decided she wanted to change her last name. "I'm tired of being plain old Patricia Jackson" she complained. "I want a glamorous name, like Joan Crawford or Lauren Bacall." On the way through Palo Alto, we crossed Ravenswood Avenue.

"How about Ravenswood?" someone asked from the back of the van, and Patricia Jackson has been Patricia Ravenswood ever since.

Our morning at Berkeley High brought us down in a hurry. The performance there did not begin or end well. That morning, on the way to the high school with the other readers in the van, Jayda remembered she had forgotten to pick up Tina and had to go back for her. By the time they arrived, Jayda's face was grim, and Tina's eyes had a wild shine that made me uneasy. She'd done her hair up in two pigtails that stood straight up on top of her head.

"Tina, are you staying on your meds?" I asked.

"Jayda doesn't want me in the show. That's why she forgot to pick me up."

"That's not what I asked. Are you taking your meds?"

"Don't need 'em. They just make me dopey," she muttered and slouched to the other side of the stage. While we set up our equipment, groups of jostling students trailed into the auditorium, calling out to each other across rows of seats. The air smelled moist, a repellent mixture of body sweat and old bananas. There were no counselors or teachers in view that I could see; my stomach churned and the readers looked poised to bolt for the door. After some technical difficulties, the student in the sound booth signaled that he was ready to go, and I took a mike to begin my welcome speech. The auditorium stayed alive with talk. Suddenly from behind me, Jayda, formidably large in blue jeans and a black sweatshirt, grabbed the mike from my hand and strode past me to the front of the stage.

"Hey!" She glared across the rows of kids all the way to the back.

"Oh, God," I inhaled, dreading what might be coming next and folded my arms across my chest to steady myself.

"Do you know how lucky you are?" Jayda demanded. Chatter dwindled as the students stared. "I was raped when I was thirteen, had two babies, and ended up living homeless on the streets. So you listen to me. Be grateful for what you got." There was a long moment of exquisite silence before the sound booth student turned out the lights. I let out my breath, and the first slide went up on the screen.

We were nearing the end, when restlessness set in again, a rolling motion of sound that swept through the room like a squall of wind across the Bay. A group of boys in the front rows made loud comments, and I wondered where the teachers were, if we would make it through, and why I had ever accepted the invitation in the first place. A photograph of a woman, her head tilted back in laughter, was on the screen. It was Tina's piece.

Good news today!
I feel good news coming.
Maybe I can allow myself out of this bondage
That I carry like a ball and chain

Good news today! I feel it's coming!...

She was opening her mouth to start the next line when a voice called out, "It'll be good news when this thing is over," and students around him hooted with laughter. Tina was done with that. She threw down her script and stomped to the edge of the stage where she fixed furiously on the first few rows. The bright light from the projector turned her two pigtails into a shadow of devil's horns behind her. "You guys down there, you, the ones being so smart assed. You know where you're going to end up? Out on the Avenue sucking dick, that's where."

Berkeley High was Tina's last show.

The Lonely Years

Mother's increasing isolation at 596 after Dad's death was a constant worry. Now in her late eighties, she varied somewhere between borderline forgetfulness and full-blown dementia. All mixed together with a broken heart.

Her mourning for my own dad took the form of rehearsing other heartbreaks when she was young. Her favorite story was telling again and again the agony she had felt at her mother's death from a brain tumor when Mother was only fourteen, and then her father's immediate second marriage to a cold, unfeeling stepmother. They were equally painful to hear. She swallowed her grief with a turned head, a half laugh of apology for tears. Like her, I sometimes thought that if I let myself cry, I might never stop.

My visits always brought me face to face with life at 596 as it had been since the '40s. The lack of central heating meant that every morning a gas heater in each room had to be lit with kitchen matches to bring the house to a bearable temperature. This woefully inadequate arrangement kept Mother in a state of petulant neediness; her internal temperature gauge became increasingly erratic, and she couldn't tell that by afternoon the house had become unbearably hot. "It's freezing in here" was one of her favorite refrains. When her bedroom wall heater stopped working completely, James had to call a man to extract what turned out to be a dead rat stuck somewhere down the flue.

Constantly trying to solve things, I made plans. Order a central heater with a thermostat, order a new stove from Sears. But I knew it was all for naught. A day later she wouldn't understand how they worked, why I needed to meddle, and why anything had to be different from the way it was. Once,

I asked Mother if she didn't think it was time to get rid of Waltzing Matilda, the house trailer. "I like to know I had a past," she replied briefly, and then endeared herself to me by launching unexpectedly into song.

> *Ho! Boys ho! To California go!*
> *There's plenty of gold so we've been told*
> *On the banks of the Sacramento.*

"My goodness, where did that come from?" She laughed at herself. "Isn't old age funny? There's a surprise around every corner."

I had a sudden guilty memory of how, long ago, I had foisted three kids onto her for two weeks so Parks and I could go to the Bahamas with his parents. Bitsy had come down with chicken pox the first day. "Mom, you're great," I said. And meant it.

Meanwhile, James struggled with a foot disabled by diabetes as well as uneven blood sugar so that his temper under the best of circumstances was fragile. Without Dad to look after, he increased his efforts to solve Mother's consuming neediness. The more he hovered, the more helpless she felt, and the more dictatorial she became until he exploded from the sheer frustration of it all. Geneen reported that on one such occasion he flew into a rage and yelled, "You're a dreadful person, Mrs. Lewis, and Mr. Lewis thought so too." By the time I had made up my mind to fire him, Mother couldn't remember anything had happened, and said, "I wouldn't dream of letting him go."

I missed Annie. My kids visited their grandmother when they could, but they had their own lives. Liz was managing her farm in Wisconsin; Rosie worked and lived in Portland with her husband; and Mac was immersed in his San Franciso law practice. My brother Thad made an effort to help, but Mother's idiosyncratic aging stretched his patience to the edge of what he could endure. They had not been on the best of terms since his second marriage to a strong-willed wife soon after the death of his first wife five years before from cancer. Not surprisingly, the new wife clashed with Mother, and Thad, caught in the middle, came less often. My emotions fluctuated as well, and I ricocheted from one contrast to the next, from one role to the next, never sure who I was. Child to adult, mother to daughter, and back again. And so it cycled.

James insisted on meeting my plane each time I arrived. Standing on the curb in the white Burbank sun, I would steel myself as his Cadillac loomed into view, his forehead barely visible above the dashboard. During the drives home, he would fill me in on the burdens of his life. On one of my annual Christmas trips, he delivered a flood of non-information in response to my invitation to join Mother and me for Christmas dinner.

"No, Hon, I won't be having dinner with you, thank you, you're always so generous, but since I don't have family, I was thinking I'd like to go to Vegas, but Hon, if you want me to stay, of course, I'm never one to shirk my duties, but I don't remember when I've had any time off…" His jowls jiggled as he talked, and I let my thoughts wander out the car window to the parched, sage-covered hills as we made our way back to Mother and the house. I thought about persuading her to move to Berkeley; then I tried to imagine moving back to Altadena with her. Each time, my mind went blank.

I thought about Jayda back home, her generous hug when we said goodbye, her voice on the phone when I called her to vent into a sympathetic ear. "Next time," she said, "Let's drive down so I can meet your mom," but my imagination couldn't stretch that far. I tried to picture Jayda appearing in the study door, her arms spread open to Mother who would rise shakily from her chair to respond. No matter how much I might remind Mother, I was afraid she would confuse Jayda with someone she had hired to clean. And I couldn't trust James who had once referred to an Arabian man on TV as "a camel jockey." Jayda would certainly want to cross the street, where she could camp out on the bleachers and watch the games. I would want to go, too.

Scenes from the Road

Geneen reassured me that, in spite of my worries, everything was going smoothly at 596 and that I should take some time away. Go somewhere. Anywhere. I relaxed into a vision of myself on a road trip, free of cares, driving through high desert on an endless road, disappearing into something new.

Jayda could go with me, I thought. It would be fun to show her new places. I had been privileged to be able to travel; now she would have the chance to do the same. Maybe I was looking for new excitement, for a chance to take risks after living carefully for so long. Maybe it would be a way to test our soul connection.

At first, when I asked her, she was anxious. Where would we stay? How long would we be gone? What if there were bugs? She was terrified of bugs. Any bugs. Even butterflies. But the more I described two to three weeks filled with the dramatic beauty of the Eastern Sierra down Rt. 395, the open vistas of Death Valley, Nevada, and Navajoland, the more she wanted to go. I thought the road trip was going to be all about Jayda. It turned out to be more about me.

The day before we left, we packed my station wagon with camping gear I had unearthed, an ice chest, road maps, and duffel bags of clothes. Jayda had appointed herself keeper of my camera bag and tripod, and laid them carefully on the backseat. Straightening up, she gave me a long look. Her dyed hair, cut short, shone blonde in the afternoon sun. "I'm gonna bring a gun."

"You're what?'

"I'm bringin' a gun."

"Yeah, sure." I stood back, hands on hips. "And I'm bringing a hand grenade."

"I'm not kidding."

"A loaded gun?"

"Why would I bring an unloaded gun?"

"Why bring any gun? We're perfectly safe."

"Hey," she said, "You have no clue what's out there, do you? If we're going to camp, it's not safe. Someone could get us. We need a gun."

I folded my arms across my chest with growing alarm, imagining a small silver handgun tucked under the front seat. Or perhaps a suspicious bulge on the side of her duffel. Easily within reach. "For heaven's sake, Jayda, camping is perfectly safe. And there is no way you're going to bring a gun in the car. It's illegal and it's dangerous. Since when do you own a gun?" Here was a side of Jayda I hadn't seen before.

"I know people. I can get one." She stared at her Nikes in sulky defiance, drawing circles on the driveway with her toe. I stood my ground. Finally, she muttered. "I don't care what you say, at least I'm bringing mace. You can't stop me from bringing mace." I didn't know what mace looked like or how to use it, but it made me think of curry powder or nutmeg, warm like her skin. At least it wasn't a gun. My tone softened.

"Fine, if you want to bring mace, bring mace, and if it'll make you feel better, I promise, we don't have to camp all the time. We can stay in motels as much as you want." I sighed. Half the fun of road tripping was camping. And how will I know for sure if she has left the gun behind?

"Man, I love to drive." Well in charge again, Jayda settled back to cruise Highway 395 south of Reno as if she owned the road, wrap-around sunglasses firmly in place. We had brought CDs of our favorite music, but Jayda didn't think much of my music like *Peter, Paul and Mary* or *100 Best Mozart*. Her choices were lesbian café singers I'd never heard of and two CDs of *Sweet Honey In the Rock*.

Months before, I had taken her and the readers to a live concert of *Sweet Honey* at Berkeley's Zellerbach Hall. Looking down from the top of the balcony next to Jayda, I had fallen in love with the five women on stage in their sumptuous African dresses swaying to rhythms that made my body tingle. Jayda reared up from her seat at the end of one number to yell, "Sweet Honey, I love you," to a packed house. Only once at the end of an opera had I felt brave enough to call out a muted "Bravo." I wondered what it must be like to feel so free, to dare to take risks. The next day, while papers blared salacious headlines about President Clinton, I thought it daring to go to Telegraph Avenue and to have my ears double-pierced.

In the passenger seat beside Jayda, one bare foot on the dashboard, my hand draped out the window in the warm air, I sang along with *Sweet Honey* as if I had grown up with it. *We are the ones, we are the ones, we've been waiting,* or *Sometimes I feel like a motherless child, a lon-n-ng way-y-y from home.* When she asked if I knew that "motherless" meant "without our home country of Africa," I nodded, pretending I'd known it all along.

Shadows were lengthening across Owens Valley when, on impulse, I turned in at a small sign on the right: MANZANAR RELOCATION CENTER. A cloud crossed the darkening sun as we drove without speaking up a deserted gravel road and stopped next to desolate rows of concrete foundations. Jayda set up the tripod for me to photograph these stark reminders of another time. The Japanese-Americans I was supposed to have interviewed for my senior Vassar thesis paper could have been imprisoned here, I thought. That Christmas, I had gotten married instead. A chill wind ruffled my shirt.

It's good to be here with Jayda, I thought. Walking beside her, I had a sudden memory of my friend Midori in our high school PE locker room five years after the war. Everyone was scrambling to change back to blouses and skirts for class. I remembered that Midori rummaged in the locker above mine, and when I leaned down to pull on my penny loafers, I saw a sharply angled scar across the back of her thigh. "Hey, Midori, where did you get that scar?" Her hand flew to cover her leg.

"From barbed wire." Her voice was barely audible. "At a camp."

"At a camp?" I was amazed. "You went to a camp that had barbed wire?" Then my face went hot when I realized she was talking about a different kind of camp.

"I'm sorry," I muttered, leaning down as if I couldn't get my shoe on.

"It's okay," Midori said. "Let's hurry or we'll be late for class."

Jayda stooped to pick up a rock, and stuck a pinch of tobacco on the ground where it had been. "The rock is to remind me about the people who were prisoners in this place," she said when she saw my questioning look. "When you take something from the land, you leave something. It's a tribal tradition. I'm a quarter Cherokee, but I don't know which quarter." She laughed. "There's enough of me to go around for all four quarters."

It was getting dark when we finally pulled into the one motel on Death Valley's rim. Pickup trucks wheeled in and out of the parking lot in front of a low-slung building with strings of lights blinking along the eves and country music pounding from the motel bar. Jayda slouched in her seat. "I'm not going in there," she said from under her baseball cap pulled half way down her face.

"There's no place else to go. I'm sorry," I said apologetically, as if it were my fault this place was so crowded. When I went inside, a plastic cactus sat on the counter where a man in a cowboy hat was backlit by a Pabst Blue Ribbon sign.

"No rooms left, lady. Nope, nothin' else nearby, the next place is 'cross the valley, a good long piece from here." I sighed, elbows on the counter. He looked at me doubtfully, scratching an unshaven chin. "I tell you what though. There's some tent cabins out back for twenty bucks. I can let you have one of those."

Thank goodness, I thought, we can camp and won't have to drive back to Lone Pine. "I'll take it," I said. Camping in a tent was second nature to me after our long-ago summers at the beach. "Right on the sand," my mother always said. She was happier next to the ocean than any place on earth, and when Mother was happy, I was happy. And safe.

"I'm not going in there," Jayda repeated when I came back to the car. "I'm not staying in any tent."

"Please, Jayda. You'll be in the tent with me. Otherwise we'll have to sleep in the car. There's no place else to go." It had been a long day on the road and I was dead tired. Once inside the tent, Jayda sat hunched on the edge of one cot, her jacket pulled up to her ears. Johnny Cash thrummed "Ring of Fire" from the bar, and we could hear the sound of muffled voices in tents on either side. Jayda refused to lie down. "I can't stay here, Mer. There's no lock on the door. What if someone comes in?"

"No one's going to come in. Trust me, it's going to be fine. It will be morning before you know it and we'll go." Rolling into a fetal position under a blanket, I put a pillow over my head and, lulled by the beat of the music, fell immediately to sleep.

I dreamed a bear was zipping and unzipping duffel bags on the floor of the tent while Jayda tossed it potato chips. In my dream, the bear was snuffling and pawing at my shoulder. I struggled onto one elbow and squinted furiously at my watch. I was never at my best when deprived of sleep.

"Jayda, listen, for God's sake. It's four o'clock in the morning. Please, will you let me sleep. Just a couple more hours."

"We gotta get out of here." Her voice rose. "I been up all night." A light from the motel office reflected the misery on her face. She had worn the same expression when she told me about the man who had come into her room when she was a kid and lain on her. Someone in her family, she had said.

"Jayda, really, it's not like when you were young," I said more gently. "No one's going to hurt you." I didn't know how to comfort her except to give her a hug. Road tripping with Jayda wasn't going to be as easy as I thought. I pulled on my sweatshirt, and zipped up my duffel. She followed me into the parking lot with her gear, and when I turned on the engine, the passenger door slammed and a mumbled "I'm sorry," came from somewhere inside her jacket. I craved only sleep followed by a steaming mug of coffee, and despaired of ever finding either again.

In the beam of our headlights, the road's center line led into dark oblivion. I kept my eyes glued to the stripe as we drove under a dome of stars, until outlines of hills, dark against darker, began to reveal themselves. I edged the car to a stop on the shoulder to yawn, rub my face and look. Never had I been up so early under depths of heavens like these. While I watched, the faintest line of light began to shape the horizon, as if God were beginning to stir. Suddenly, before I could yawn again, a bold streak of light flashed in front of us, carving the sky in half before it vanished as suddenly as it had come.

"Wow! Did you see that?" I forgot I was mad. "A comet! Did I make that up?"

A chuckle from inside the jacket. "That was no comet, Swee'Pea, that was the hand of God. You'd have missed Him if you'd stayed asleep back in that tent. Here, I'll do the driving." She came round to trade places and take the wheel. The lost child of the night was gone. The shaman Jayda was back in charge.

We started across open desert in the direction of Las Vegas, fortified by coffee and a sticky bun from a café on the valley floor. It was my turn to drive and I stopped often to photograph clouds piled on distant mountains, billowed whipped cream against azure sky. When we passed craggy formations, Jayda pointed out faces everywhere, hawk-like noses, eyes slit into rock walls, jutting chins. "They're our spirit ancestors," she said. "They watch over the land to remind us who came before." Other times, the road's brilliant yellow line invited us into vast expanses of sagebrush, where invisible lizards scuttled behind rocks. With Jayda half asleep beside me, wind blowing hot, cruise control on 75, we were the only car on the road. Euphoric, I sang softly to myself until, suddenly, my eye caught a flash of red and blue in the rear view mirror.

"Oh, shit."

"What?"

"A cop."

"You gotta be trippin'." Jayda sat up straighter and shifted sideways to look.

He was still well behind us, but he was closing the gap. "Maybe he'll pass us," I said. He didn't. I slowed to a stop on the shoulder and he pulled in behind me, dust swirling, flashers working. "Double shit." Taking out my license, I reached a shaking hand across Jayda to the glove compartment for the registration papers. The cop sat in his car, taking as much time as if he were writing a novel, until finally he sauntered towards Jayda's side of the car. "Check out this guy," I whispered. "He looks just like John Wayne." But Jayda only pulled her hat further down her face. I had a sudden image of the gun she had wanted to bring. The cop looked first at Jayda, then at me, with both his hands placed firmly on her open window. I waited for him to tell me I had been going 120 miles an hour and became excessively polite.

"Good afternoon, Officer." My pulse still pounding, I added "How are you doing, Sir?" as I handed him my papers. "You must have to drive long distances out here." He pushed his hat back and studied my license and registration.

"Lady?" He drawled at me across Jayda who gave him no more notice than a cactus. "D'you know your registration tag is out of date?"

"My what? My registration tag?" How could he have seen my license plate from that far away? "But I paid it," I stammered in relief. "Look, I'll show you." I fumbled for my purse under Jayda's feet, its strap catching on her sneaker, and ran my finger down two months of payments written into my checkbook. "There!" Triumphant, I showed him the entry: May 8, 2000, DMV Car Registration. He scratched his head again.

"Did you give 'em proof of insurance? They gotta have proof of insurance before they send you a new sticker." He pulled out his notebook and leafed through yellow carbons for a fresh sheet.

"I don't know if I did or not."

He busied himself with his notebook. "I'll have to give you a ticket. Get that registration taken care of within ten days and you won't get a fine."

"A fine? But I didn't do anything." Jayda, her face immobile, poked my thigh with a clenched knuckle. I shut up, and he handed me a ticket. With a gesture towards his hat and one more look at Jayda, he strolled back to his car, made an abrupt U turn and drove back the way he had come.

Jayda let out a scornful laugh. "He didn't give a shit about your registration. Have you ever seen a cop who came to the passenger side of the car? And stayed there? You know why he did that, don't you?"

I wiggled my license back in its slot. "Maybe he thinks you're cute."

"Cute? You kidding? It's 'cause I'm black, that's why. For all he knew, I was kidnapping you. Girl? He was gonna save your little white ass." She dug into her shirt pocket for her cigarettes. "It's a good thing I wasn't driving when he decided to earn himself some money this afternoon. He would have had a good speed chase on his hands. You wait here. I gotta have me a smoke."

Across the street from our motel, the KMart where Jayda wanted to pick up a new pair of socks was rush-hour crowded. She turned when we got to the automatic front door. "You want to see something?" she asked. "You watch what they do. They're gonna put a tail on me faster than you can blink. Maybe put one on both of us. A mixed race couple."

"You think you're going to be tailed? For heaven's sake, you're just going in there to buy some socks. We're not Bonnie and Clyde."

Jayda laughed briefly. "A big store like this? With all these white folks? I tell you what, we'll pretend I'm here by myself. You stay behind and see what happens." In a rush of chill air, we were immersed in a mixture of smells. Stale popcorn and cheap perfume. I stood close to the cash registers while Jayda ambled up an aisle with her rolling gate. She looked young and vulnerable, like a large teenage boy in a baseball hat. A mixed race couple, I thought, remembering her words. Is that what we are? A couple? As I watched, a skinny man with freckles, appeared from another aisle and fell in behind her. Like a private eye in the movies, I waited a moment, then trailed after them. When Jayda stopped to look at something, Freckles pretended to examine the contents of a shelf; I read a shampoo label. When she sauntered further up the aisle, Freckles followed and again, I took up the rear.

But at the sports department's rack of socks, our procession came to a halt when a hearty looking man in a Cougars athletics jacket stopped her with a tap on her shoulder. She turned, they talked, Jayda laughed, they talked some more, the man shrugged, clapped her on the back, and they shook hands. Was this man a security officer too? I looked around for Freckles, but he had turned into a side aisle and was heading to the front of the store. By the time I was back at the cash registers, he was unlocking a door marked Employees Only. Jayda caught up with me and pointed towards the employees' door. "That was him. Did you see him? That's the one."

"Yeah, for sure I saw him. You were right about that. But why was that man in the football jacket talking to you? What did he want?"

"Oh, him." She laughed as she paid for the socks. "He's the high school football coach in this town, wherever we are. He wanted to know if I would try out for the team."

The Grand Canyon was supposed to be a highlight of our trip, and I was excited for Jayda to see the beauty of its grandeur. I had hoped to be there in the early morning when the day was fresh and the light was soft for photography, but we got a late start and Jayda wanted to stop at every historical marker along the way. It was nearing noon by the time we found a space in the Visitor Center parking lot. We were getting out into oppressive heat, when a gleaming charter bus pulled wide around parked cars to stop behind us, wheeze open its doors, and spew its passengers onto the pavement. Behind dark glasses, tourists stretched, searched for cameras, or pushed past us to the railings to take pictures of each other or wait their turn at telescopes, three minutes for each quarter. A family group passed us. A child's voice, "Look at her, Mama!" and a woman's sharp, "Shhh! Don't stare." A teenage girl looked back at us, said something to her friend and they both laughed.

"This place is for rich people," Jayda said.

"Well, they're not all rich," I started to say, but I knew that wasn't what she meant. I was looking with new eyes, wary of insult, watchful in a peripheral way. I've dragged Jayda into White America, I thought. While she smoked, we gazed across the canyon, its walls bleached from the midday heat. A second bus, windows dark, with a sign on its windshield, SALT LAKE CITY KIWANIS CLUB, pulled in behind the first. Jayda pushed back her cap and wiped sweat with the back of her hand.

"I don't like this place." she said abruptly. "Let's go."

"We could go over to the lodge and get something cold to drink," I said, hoping to salvage something of the day.

She shook her head. "I'm not going there. Let's get out of here."

Heading north from the Grand Canyon into Navajoland, we drove for at least an hour in silence while I considered turning around for home. Jayda must have been considering her stomach. "I'm hungry. Let's eat," she said suddenly as we neared a market advertising deli sandwiches.

"Hey, whazzup?" she said to the acne-faced clerk in the shadowy cool. The teenager looked as if he'd been taking the same sandwich orders behind the same counter his whole life. He stared at Jayda and then at me without speaking. "Always this hot?" she asked conversationally, setting my camera bag on the floor and resting her middle against the case while she considered her options from a long list on the wall. The clerk folded his arms and waited. "I'll have a salami and Swiss cheese with plenty of mustard and mayo on a roll. No tomatoes." In slow motion, the kid reached in for the salami. "Oh, yeah," she added, "Put on some avocado, would you?" He looked at her, salami half way out of the case.

"You want avocado? That'll be thirty-five cents extra if you want avocado." Jayda snorted and fumbled for her wallet.

"He wouldn't have said that about extra money to you," she said to me over her shoulder. "He doesn't think I can pay."

The clerk flushed. "Oh, you guys together? Sorry 'bout that." He pulled out the cheese.

"That's right," said Jayda with her big smile. "As a matter of fact, this lady with me is a famous photographer and I'm her assistant. You can add a Diet Pepsi and some chips. I'll pay for those too."

We ate driving through endless scrub and amusing ourselves by imagining what more we could have said to rattle the clerk. Or how we could turn ourselves into Bonnie and Clyde. "We'll choose only upscale stores in large towns," said Jayda. "I'll hold the car out front, while you take stuff off racks. You could get away with it. Then you'll jump into the car and I'll drive us away."

"I'll have fancy clothes and a monogrammed handbag," I said. "We'll be the terrors of the West."

"You'd never have the nerve." She grinned.

"Hey, don't underestimate me. Do you want to hear one of the songs we used to sing at college?" I breathed through my nose in my best Eartha Kitt. "I want to be e-e-e-vil, I want to be ba-a-a-d." Jayda leaned back, laughing until her hat fell off.

"Yeah, Swee'Pea, that's you all right, e-e-e-vil and ba-a-a-d."

"Don't knock it. Once I was so scared I'd fail an organic chemistry test, I wrote formulas on a paper and hid it in my glasses case."

"Now that's what I call criminal, Baby Girl." Laughter made her dimples disappear into her round cheeks, and when she called me Baby Girl it made me feel desirable, like someone who dared to be different instead of always living by the book. "I need a hit," said Jayda suddenly. I was used to her smoking joints, even welcomed them to calm her when she got nervous or her back hurt. I pulled over to the side of the road where she balanced a square of paper on her knee, sprinkled marijuana leaves from a sandwich bag and rolled it between her fingers. She dampened one edge to seal it and took a deep drag.

"It smells sweet," I said, "Like wet eucalyptus leaves." She offered the joint to me, but I shook my head. The smoke made me cough.

"I used to do crack," she said casually as she took another drag, "But I been clean thirteen years."

It was the first I'd heard she had ever used crack, but I was distracted by the map and thirteen years seemed a long time ago. "How'd you stop?"

"I don't know." Her voice trailed off. "I guess I just got tired of it and quit. It's a lot easier to quit crack than cigarettes."A sharp-eared bunny ran out of a clump of tumbleweed, stopped rigid on its hind legs, and vanished as quickly as it had come.

We found a motel behind a Walmart, and when I checked in, a tall man pushed aside a beaded curtain and looked at me, neither welcoming nor unwelcoming. I tried not to stare at the neat crisscross wrapping of the turban he wore. A Sikh probably. "Two double beds, please," I told him. "My friend is waiting in the car."

"I have no double rooms, only one queen." I settled for the one with the queen, and without expression, he handed me the key. Swinging her duffel off her shoulder, Jayda sat heavily on the motel's chenille bedspread and flicked on the TV. Only then did she look around. "Are you crazy? You took a room with only one bed for two women? You know what he's gonna think, don't you? Lesbians, that's what he's gonna think. Do you know how dangerous that is? Aww, shit, girl."

I laughed. "Aww, shit, Jayda. That guy isn't going to think anything. He's got enough problems of his own being a Sikh out here." The hell with it, I thought, I was tired of what people might think, and rummaged in my suitcase for a clean T-shirt without success. "Listen, I'm going to run over to that Walmart and pick up a new shirt. D'you want to come?" She shook her head, her eyes on the screen.

Glad to be on my own for a change, I threaded my way in my dog-eared sandals across a vacant lot behind the motel to the entrance of the store. Once inside, I paused to check out the scene, the security guard, and other customers. I found a table of T-shirts and chose two in size medium. I wanted to get one for Jayda, but the biggest was only an XL, way too small for her. Tensely watchful, I started for the cash registers, when I had a sudden realization. Jayda wasn't with me. There was no one for the other customers to stare at, to wonder about, to make fun of. The strain went out of my shoulders. My body relaxed. I don't have to be on my guard, I thought. Just for a moment, I had a glimmer of what it must be like to be in Jayda's shoes, to be a black woman in a place where nearly everyone else is white.

Jayda was still hunched in front of the TV when I got back with the shirts and some sandwiches I bought at Subway. Barefoot, I settled on the front stoop with my legs stretched out, to drink wine from a plastic motel cup and watch the lowering sun. Peace settled over me as sounds from the TV drifted faintly through the open door and then, under the cloak of dusk, Jayda plumped down next to me, a soda in one hand. After a moment, she began to sing, soft and caressing.

As I went down in the river to pray
Studying about that good old way
And who shall wear the starry crown
Good Lord, show me the way.

Something deep stirred in me and I leaned against her, the length of our legs touching, humming the refrains. She knew all the verses.

O sisters, let's go down
Let's go down, come on down
O sisters, let's go down...
Down in the river to pray

O brothers, let's go down
Let's go down, come on down...

When at last her voice died away, we sat comfortably, letting our thoughts drift across the parked cars and into the night sky broken by a sliver of moon. Later, curled under the chenille bedspread, back to back, warmth to warmth, we slept.

The next morning, we drove for miles through desert that turned different shades of white. I had found instant coffee in the deserted motel office, but there had been nowhere on the empty road for breakfast. Jayda was at ease now that we'd crossed into the Navajo Nation and we held hands while she drove. I watched sheep wander around scattered houses, mongrel dogs smell the roadside and children play by doorways, looking up without expression as we went by. I longed to photograph them, but knew better than to stop.

Cafe Open. A sign blinked in one dirty window of a store set back from the road. "I'm starving." Jayda braked onto the shoulder and pulled the car around. I looked doubtfully at the café where a scruffy dog scratched its stomach by the door with no apparent relief.

"This doesn't look great," I objected. "Let's go a little further, there's bound to be a small town up ahead." This cafe belonged to locals, the kind of place I didn't want to stop for fear of intruding where I didn't belong.

"We're going here," she said with her usual determination. Inside, naugahyde stools at a counter held one lone Navajo customer, his face partially hidden by a cowboy hat. "Whazzup," she greeted the man. Gone was the Jayda who slouched under her cap. Here she was at home. Glancing at us with none of the suspicious surprise we were used to, he nodded towards a curtain behind the counter. A teenage girl wearing glasses on a stolid face emerged after a moment and wrote our order on a small pad. While we waited, we looked more closely at artwork hung at random on the walls. Butterflies, rainbows, garden scenes—they had a folk art quality we both liked. The waitress was back with our coffee. "Who did the paintings on the wall?" I asked. Her face lit up.

"My brother. Do you want to meet him?" She called to someone, and in a moment, a young man in a T-shirt and jeans, his hair fastened in a ponytail long down his back, pushed open the curtain. He acknowledged us shyly.

"I have a few more out back if you want to see them. I'm Moogie." A gentle invitation, not a tourist pitch. When we finished eating, we followed him along a brushy path to an airstream trailer. "Please." He gestured towards the door and followed us up a step into a crowded space where art supplies filled a card table. An air conditioner whined. I wouldn't be here, I thought, if it weren't for Jayda. A woman, drying her hands on a towel, glanced up. "This is my wife, Doli," Moogie said. "Her name means blue bird."

Doli smiled. "Moogie's name means love for a grandmother. When he was little, he called his grandmother Moogie, and before she passed, she gave him back the name." Our host leafed through pastels leaning against the wall until my eye caught a simple woven bowl against a luminous background. We settled on a price and he wrapped the drawing carefully in newspaper. Now, twenty years later, Moogie's framed pastel bowl still hangs on my living room wall.

My eyes wandered to a snapshot on the refrigerator door. A young Navajo girl was crouched in a twisted position on the floor. "That's our niece," said Moogie. "She was born that way. She has to crawl. Like a crab." He took the photo down to show us. "Uranium water. Our people drank it, so did the animals. The government said it didn't cause birth defects, but we know different." My people did this, I thought. The ones who make the rules, the ones who pretend things are different than they are. I remembered reading stories about uranium water years ago, but I hadn't paid attention.

When we left, we hugged each of them in turn. Back in the car, we were quiet for a long moment. "By the way," I said finally, "What does *your* name mean?"

Jayda chuckled. "I wasn't going to tell them." She put her hand on my thigh. "It means Hot Mama."

"Oh, come on. It does not." I blushed unexpectedly.

"Oh, yes, it does. Ask anyone in my family. It means I'm a Hot Mama."

We were heading north from Yellowstone across a vast expanse of plain when we saw them. At first, they looked like a line of dots against the horizon heading across Montana away from us. Closer, we could hear the hum of engines, see flashes of metal in the sun and recognize a line of motorcycles stretching as far as we could see. "Look at that. It's one of those motorcycle clubs," I said. "I'm glad they're going the other direction." Men on motorcycles made me nervous, aliens under helmets, mirrored dark glasses, bellies protruding from under leather jackets that could be hiding guns.

"I used to have a motorcycle when I worked in steel," said Jayda when they disappeared from sight. "When I had money. After the accident, I had to sell it to get the cash. Man, I loved that bike." That would be different, I thought. What would it be like to ride close behind Jayda, my arms around her broad back, the sun and wind in my face, the pavement a blur of speed under the wheels?

By the time we reached Highway 90 and turned west, it was late, time to stop after a long day. But at the first town, another band of motorcycles had invaded the motel strip and *No Vacancy* signs blinked everywhere. "Let's go," I said. "I don't want to stay here even if we could find a place. It isn't safe." But across the street, a Holiday Inn flashed a *Vacancy* sign. As if she hadn't heard me, Jayda turned directly into the driveway next to a group of Harley Davidsons. "Let's go," I repeated more loudly.

"We're going to be fine, Girlfriend. Trust me." And she was the first out of the car, greeting a group of men leaning on their bikes as if she were in her own church. We both had an inner compass that pointed to our comfort zones. I remembered the homeless park in Oakland where we often went to photograph, and where she moved easily around, shielding me like a St. Bernard guarding a child.

"Hey, Bro. Whazzup, Dude?" After I checked in, I found her leaning against the fender of the car, smoking and joking with the men. One of them offered me a beer and, except for a new growth of beard, he looked like any well-paid professional out of my past. He was, it turned out, a lawyer from Seattle.

"What'd I tell you," Jayda said when we were in our room. "They're just folks, like you and me."

I had to laugh again at the thought of the two of us. "Don't kid yourself. There's nobody anywhere just like you and me."

We'd been driving a long time. "I'm not stopping in Idaho," Jayda said suddenly in a flat tone. "We shoulda stayed where we were."

"What do you mean you're not stopping in Idaho? Where are we now?" She pushed her finger down the map to a spot in Montana about an inch from the Idaho border. "There." I took my eyes off the road long enough to follow.

"It's almost dark, and I'm bushed," I complained. "There's no place to stay now in Montana unless we go a long way back. Why didn't you tell me you didn't want to stop in Idaho?" I berated myself for not planning ahead, for not talking to Jayda earlier about where we might stay. "What's wrong with Idaho?"

"What's wrong with *you*? Everyone knows Idaho's where Nazi skinheads hang out. It's their headquarters. You think I'm staying anywhere in Idaho? Girl, you're crazy."

"A border is only a line on a map. It doesn't divide bad people from good people. We'll just stop, no one will see us, and we'll leave early in the morning. I promise."

"If you want to get killed, go ahead. I'm not stopping." She slouched in her seat, her jaw fixed. "They're looking for people like me."

A sign, *Welcome to Idaho*, shone blue in our headlights. I figured we had about eighty miles to go before we were in the state of Washington. "Well, at least you picked the small end of the state," I tried to joke. We drove in silence until at last, starting down a long, winding mountain summit, we could see the distant lights of the town of Coeur d'Alene.

"That's a stupid name for a town," grumbled Jayda. She folded her arms across her chest. Suddenly we heard a pick-up behind us, the kind with wide tail pipes. It revved its engines and pulled along side us. Out of the corner of my eye, I saw a woman's face, tight under frizzy hair, stare at us through the passenger window, then turn to say something to the driver. I speeded up, the truck speeded up, and when I slowed, the driver kept pace with us. The woman was laughing. My hands tightened on the steering wheel while Jayda fingered an unlit cigarette. "Shit," she grunted. She was right, I thought, we should have stayed in Montana. In vain, I searched the rearview mirror for the comforting lights of other cars on the road. The truck gunned its engine, pulled forward and swerved into our lane. I braked, he moved back into his own lane then swerved over again.

"Look," I said. "The first Coeur d'Alene exit. Maybe they'll turn in there." But we passed the first exit, then the second while the pick-up stuck with us, dropping back only to crowd in so close behind us that in the glare of his headlights, I was momentarily blinded. Finally, they turned at the last Coeur d'Alene exit, and with one long, accusing blast on their horn, they disappeared. When I was sure they weren't coming back, my fingers loosened their grip just as a sign loomed out of the darkness. *Welcome to Washington The Evergreen State.*

"I gotta get some weed in Spokane," said Jayda the next morning while we ate breakfast at a diner down the street from our motel. I looked up in annoyance. I didn't want to stop. Highway 90 made a straight shot through Spokane heading towards Oregon and the Columbia River. We had planned to spend a night with my daughter Rosie and her husband in Portland, and then I wanted to go home.

"You don't know anyone in Spokane. How are you going to get marijuana there?"

"I don't need to know someone. There are ways. It won't take long. Trust me, we'll be fine." Jayda was driving and she took the last Spokane exit, where blocks of traffic, billboards and stoplights were jarring after the meditative monotony of the freeway. Another mile and a few blocks to the left, the city seemed greyer and emptier with every low-slung apartment we passed.

"This doesn't feel good," I said uneasily, but I was curious too about what Jayda would do next. In the middle of one block, a youngish-looking man lounged against a telephone pole and idly watched us go by. Jayda circled the block and came back, making sure the man was still there before she eased to the curb a half block ahead of him.

"You take the wheel, okay?" she said, getting out of the car. Glad to have control over something, I climbed into the driver's seat and rolled up the window.

"This place is creepy. Let's get out of here," I said, but Jayda was already walking down the sidewalk as if she were taking a stroll in the park. This is no longer an adventure, I scolded myself. We're Bonnie and Clyde all right, but I'm not supposed to be the one at the wheel. A feral-looking cat darted across the street, and I wiped my palms, damp now, on the front of my jeans. In the rear view mirror, Jayda's back blocked my view of the man, but I could see her head nodding. In a moment, the man had disappeared around the corner and she was back in the car.

"He's got it. He said to wait ten minutes then we'll meet him two blocks ahead. He said not to stop, he'd hand it to me, and if we drove straight, we'd pick up the freeway in six blocks."

"Jayda, we absolutely should not be here. How do we know that guy's not an undercover cop?"

"Don't worry, he's not a cop."

"How do you know?"

"I just know." We sat. I looked at my watch feeling irritated with Jayda and even more irritated with myself for giving in to this situation.

"We'll give it two more minutes and then we're done," I said. Finally, starting the engine, I waited for a bus to pass, pulled into the street and drove slowly, my eyes scanning for what I was sure would be flashing red and blue lights.

"That's him," said Jayda. "On the corner." I slowed the car to a crawl, the man reached into his jacket, and in the flash of a moment, handed a paper bag to Jayda that she stuck under the seat. Holding my breath, I stepped on the accelerator, being careful to keep the speedometer under twenty-five, and exhaled with relief when a green I-90 sign angled into view on the left. Safely on the freeway, Jayda pulled out the bag and rubbed a pinch of leaves between her fingers. She smelled deeply.

"Fuck!"

"What?"

She smelled again. "There goes nothing."

"What?"

"It's a fucking bag of tea."

I couldn't stop laughing. "Don't you think it's time to go home?"

She stared at the contents of the bag. "Yeah," she said finally, throwing the bag on the floor with a snort of a chuckle. "Yeah, I guess it is."

In the Jail

After the road trip, it was a relief to be home where I could slip comfortably back into my familiar routine and my own white America. There was Mother to visit and worry about, friends to see, photography classes and writing groups to catch up on. Nonetheless, I knew that my life was not the same. Jayda and I had come back with a deeper connection and a new intimacy we had not had before. Her family and her friends like Lawanda took it for granted that we were a couple, while most of my own friends, while cordial, seemed hesitant to accept my love for this financially broke, undeniably young black woman.

It was good to be back volunteering at the Drop-In, where there was so much laughter and sisterly conversation. I felt naturally drawn to the open friendliness of the black community, as if I had lived as an African American woman in another life. At the same time, by becoming a couple with Jayda, I was unquestionably out of my comfort zone as I tried to straddle two worlds with a foot in each: my life in my white community, and my life with Jayda, her family, and our shared creativity in the Sisters Project.

I didn't tell anyone when Jayda and I went to *Good Vibrations*, a popular adult shop on San Pablo Avenue. I was nervous at the thought of the incredulous expressions on faces when we walked in, but to my surprise, no one so much as glanced at us. We could easily have wandered into the cosmetics department of Nordstrom's except that the merchandise was different. Love comes in all ages and shapes, I said to myself. Right? Maybe we weren't so unusual a couple after all, I told myself firmly; I tried to ignore a faint sense of unease about what I was doing and what Jayda might be thinking about our future.

Over time, safe in the security of our twosome, Jayda stopped disappearing and had fewer bouts of depression. But always out of money, she moved from one living situation to the next, hinting broadly each time that she wanted to move in with me. And, fiercely protective of my independence, I hinted just as broadly that she couldn't. At the same time, I loved her closeness, and was proud of our unique relationship. She sometimes threatened to bolt from the Project when she was anxious or her back hurt too much. Determined to keep the Project going, I wanted her to feel safe. In this frame of mind, we continued our work together.

I'd never been inside a jail, much less been responsible for a group performing there. When we were invited to do a show at the SF Women's Detention Center, I was as nervous as everyone else. On the appointed evening, our group waited outside the women's jail on a fog-cold sidewalk, shivering and yawning. Everyone wore matching black T-shirts that my assistant, Theresa, had designed for them with Sisters Project lettered in white across their fronts and Shadow Voices across their backs. But I had been reassured when Lawanda agreed to come with us for moral support. Her comfortable presence always put me at ease. "I'll come with you this once," she said, "But you don't need me. You are already doing God's work."

I set down the projector I was carrying, and took up my role as schoolteacher. "Okay, everyone. Do you all have your IDs with pictures? And your Social Security cards?" The woman in charge had been clear on the phone that everyone had to bring two kinds of identification.

A whine from Brittany. "Mer, I forgot my social security card." She had one arm around Jayda's son, John, and the other hand braced on the small of her back. "I'm in so much pain. I put my back out this morning picking up the baby. I can't hardly stand." To no one's surprise, she and John had gotten married in Las Vegas and had a baby boy. I thought she was going to cry.

"Oh, shit, Brittany," I said wearily. We'd already blown it and we weren't even inside.

"Oh, shit, Brittany," echoed Jayda. Taking a deep breath, I rang the buzzer next to the heavy security door and was confronted by a broad shouldered guard with a wide, Slavic face. She shook her head when I told her we were missing a Social Security card.

"No card. No entry. She waits outside. That's the rules."

I looked at Lawanda for reinforcement. Pushing through our milling throng, she presented herself to the guard. "I'm a minister," she said, which wasn't true. "I will vouch for Brittany personally. You have my word and that of the Lord God Almighty." My eyes widened in admiration. Lawanda could sound holier than the Bible itself when she put her mind to it.

"Huh," said the woman, glaring at us before turning her back and whispering into an intercom. "All right," she said, reluctantly. "The super says okay, but she'll have to be frisked. You follow me and nobody talk."

"Frisked?" I asked anxiously. I felt especially responsible for young Brittany.

"Not body searched." The Slavic woman dripped scorn. "Just frisked." We filed into a stark hallway, through another locked door, and down another hall to a bare room, where the woman patted Brittany up one side and down the other. At least we were in. A second guard, a friendlier black woman, escorted us through a third locked door into a large room where folding metal chairs had been set up in rows near where we stood. A wide balcony above us with a waist-high railing circled half the room where several uniformed women guards wandered up and down.

Below them in the room, some fifty young women, many of them no older than Brittany, sat at long tables eating chocolate cake off paper plates, a special treat, we were told, in honor of our visit. They looked blankly at our readers. The readers stared back while Jayda and I set up microphones, and the guards in the balcony gossiped among themselves or scolded someone at the table for talking too loud. I wondered what these young women thought about us coming into this place from the outside world.

"They're so young. What are they here for?" I asked our escort.

"Mostly theft, stealing money for drugs, that kind of thing." Where had they come from, I wondered, as I watched them. What would happen to them? With a command from one of the guards, the women got up from the table, tossed their plates in a trash can, and chose chairs as far back as possible. There they sat, restless and waiting for us to prove ourselves. The readers took their places and Brittany, clutching her back with both hands, looked as if she were about to fall off her stool.

Holding the mike, I was opening my mouth to introduce everyone when Lawanda interrupted, took my elbow and pointed me firmly towards a chair. Walking straight into the light of the projector, she raised her arms and half closed her eyes. "Lord Jesus, we thank you for these women, your sacred children." She stopped to look around with her huge smile, and a hush fell over the room. Even the guards leaned over the railing to listen. "Blessed are we all to be together in this place, this sanctuary of God, for surely all places on earth are sanctuaries of God." I don't remember the rest of the prayer, but I do remember my tension easing and that I was smiling and nodding at Jayda. "You are God's beloved children," Lawanda went on, including everyone in the room with one sweeping glance. Maybe she's a minister after all, I thought.

"Thank you, Jesus," said someone in the back. "A-a-a-men," said someone else.

The prayer over, a guard switched off the lights over the chairs and I projected the opening slide on the screen. Image followed image, poem followed poem. The silence was palpable, as if everyone had stopped breathing. Even the guards. Then an image of an intense looking woman holding a small boy lit up the screen. It was Mona's turn.

This is my child! Mine.
See? This child is all
I got left of my self.
At night, I hold onto him tight
So he won't slip away out of my sight.
My child. Mine.

Without warning, in a middle row, a voice wailed, a chair crashed backwards, and a young woman pushed her way to the back of the room. Faster than I would have thought possible, Lawanda was on her feet, jogging past the rows of chairs to the sobbing woman, put her arm around her shoulders and led her to the back of the room where she held her close.

Jayda looked over at me with a worried shake of her head and I nodded. She's right, we're crazy to be doing this. We are playing with the emotions of vulnerable women on the edge. At the very least, we should bring a professional counselor with us to a show like this. But when the last slide finished and the music died away, the women were out of their chairs, clapping and stomping their feet. In the balcony above us, even the grimmest looking guard was applauding. Everyone clustered around the readers, hugging and chattering like any group of young women having a good time together.

"Thank you for coming," said the friendly guard as she walked us to the door.

"But what about the girl who was crying? Don't you think it's too much for some of them?"

"Aw, She'll be okay. They've been through a lot and they've got a lot of stuff inside they gotta get out, but they're tough. I hope you'll come again." Later she wrote us a note inviting us back: *The women were truly blessed by your efforts. You cannot imagine how much you all touched their lives.*

End of An Era

Whenever I was at 596, the familiar smells, the call of a mourning dove, the shouts from the baseball game across the street, the way the study door stuck for a moment before I pushed it open, all brought back the sweetly painful nostalgia of growing up. I didn't want to be there, but at the same time, I didn't want any of it to go away.

"Oh, dear, when will I see you again?" Mother asked after each visit as I was getting ready to leave.

"Soon, Mom, very soon," I answered, loving and cheerful. Each time, as James backed the Cadillac up the driveway to the street, past Mother's shaded succulent garden and Waltzing Matilda, sagging now on one flat tire, I leaned out the window to wave. And each time, my heart ached as she stood alone on the deck with one hand on her wheeled walker, the other waving goodbye.

One Sunday, there was a message on my answering machine when I came home from playing tennis at the Rose Garden. "Hello, dear, this is Geneen." I crossed my fingers and waited. Maybe Mother's bowels had moved and she was doing better now. Or maybe her new dog, a horrid little Pekingese that kept running away, had been found. But Geneen's sweetly melodious voice went on, "Your mother has gone to Heaven."

What? I sank onto the kitchen stool and listened to the message again while I stared at the funny cartoon I had once tacked above the phone of a small stick figure jumping up and down, pointing at the answering machine and shouting, *No messages and you die.*

Died? Did Geneen say my mother had died? Other mothers die. Not mine. I had been there only last week. I had just been with her those hot afternoons at the backyard pool when she lowered her shriveled little body in its heavy cotton bathing suit into the warm water and paddled back and forth across the shallow end five times. The tiles at the edge of the water were layered with scum from lack of care. We counted the laps. Five times. "Great, Mom! You're going to live to be a hundred."

"Ha!" she had said in disbelief, and she'd been right. She was ninety-one when she died.

"Do you want to see her?" asked Geneen when I returned her call.

"No," I said loudly. I couldn't bear the idea of my last memory of my mom being a mask of death. When I drove down the next day, Geneen had to tell the minute details over and over again. Then she wanted to tell the story of her own mother's death. More than once. It's universal, the need to tell our own mother's story when someone loses theirs. Our mothers. Our beginnings. We tell about them again and again.

I reviewed my guilt endlessly. Always rushing. Always on the move. Why hadn't I called her more often? Why hadn't I stayed the last time? Why couldn't I just hang out? But I couldn't and I didn't. I was too afraid she would swallow me up, that I would simply disappear into her well of loneliness, impatience and despair. It had to be the way it was.

Thad came to do what he could to help, and Rosie and Dan came down from Portland. I moved numbly through the inevitable tasks: cleaning, sorting, and throwing away until 596, the family's home base for over fifty years, was nothing but a shell. The rooms echoed with loneliness, and having arranged for the bank to sell the house, I later wished I had made myself visit each room to say goodbye. But I couldn't. With my feelings tightly buttoned into an emotional straight jacket, my mind felt as empty as the house when we drove away with the few belongings I had chosen to keep. We passed Gladys-the-Buick in her new home in a neighbor's driveway, and on our way to the freeway, I spotted Waltzing Matilda in the backyard of Jesús, the gardener. He had wanted the trailer for his son to have a place to sleep.

Mother would never have wanted a memorial service. Besides, I realized sadly, most of her friends had died. So it was only family, together with Geneen and James, that gathered many months later for a sunny picnic on a Santa Barbara beach. Except for two gold boxes of ashes and a collection of photographs of Mother and Dad, we didn't look anything like a memorial service as we sat in a crosslegged circle on the sand eating lunch from a nearby deli and telling stories that made us laugh. Afterwards, we waded into the waves and threw out handfuls of ashes, letting the wind blow them back into our faces and stick them to our shirts. Brushing ourselves off, we stood for a long time, knee deep in the shallows with our arms around each other, and watched Mother and Dad float away into the world that Mother had loved.

First Class to New York

The invitation came the day after Jayda and I had been arguing about how much she was using the Project van. I could hear my kitchen phone from the backyard and caught it just before it switched over to the answering machine. A man with a British accent introduced himself as Richard something and asked to speak with Jayda Jackson.

"Jayda Jackson doesn't live here," I said with sudden suspicion, breathing hard after my run. Was Jayda telling people she lived with me? She was apartment hunting again and I had vigorously held off her not-so veiled suggestions to move in with me. "Where did you get this phone number?"

"I saw a poem in a magazine that listed a number for a group called the Sisters Project. I lo-o-ved her poem, I want her to come to New York." Richard drew out the word "loved" as if she'd written it just for him. "Do you know it? It was with a photograph. A photograph of an Indian woman." He started to read,

There once was a time
When spirits roamed free...

Of course I knew it. By heart. Jayda had written it for the photo I'd taken of a Native-American woman with a gentle smile and a breeze blowing her hair across her face. Richard rushed on. "So, I'm giving a black tie dinner on Park Avenue next month to promote my wine business. The minute I read that poem, I knew the theme for the dinner had to be about Indians."

"Really?" What was he talking about?

"Yes!" He was nearly sputtering with entrepreneurial excitement. "I know some real Indian dancers from New

Jersey." What, I wondered, did "real Indians" have to do with the promotion of a wine business? This guy must be some kind of a kook. There was no way Jayda could do this. Certainly not alone. She'd never been to a formal dinner that I knew of, much less flown in an airplane.

"She could never make the trip by herself," I said firmly.

"No problem. You come with her if you want, all expenses paid." Pondering this largesse, I felt a wave of excitement. A chance to go to New York!

"Well, Jayda's sort of heavy. I don't think she'd fit in economy..." My voice trailed off.

"No problem," he repeated, "You'll fly first class. Just send me the bill and I'll send you all the information you need." When I looked him up online, his organization did seem to be for real, and despite my misgivings, the offer was too good to turn down. Like the road trip, Jayda hesitated at first. What would she wear? Who was going to be there? How many poems would she have to read? But gradually she warmed to the idea. Could we see the MTV studios on Times Square? Could we go to the top of the Empire State Building? Before long, I had made hotel reservations and we had gone shopping for clothes.

The first day in New York passed in a blur of exhausting sightseeing, and the day of the dinner, both of us were jittery with anxiety. Jayda self-medicated whenever she could, even rolling a joint in a corner park after announcing New York was too crowded and she wanted to go home. What if at the last minute, she refused to go to the dinner? Finally, I agreed to a bus trip to Harlem to pass the hours and calm our nerves. I had never been to Harlem except to peer through the window when the train to Vassar had stopped at 125th Street.

From the Lexington Avenue bus, I watched the staid elegance of upscale New York fade into a jumble of small cafes and shops with clothes and household wares on sidewalk racks. Neighborhoods became racially mixed, and snatches of salsa music drifted into the bus whenever the driver opened the door. "This is like going home," Jayda said. "This is good."

"Yes," I said, feeling myself relax. "This is good." At the end of the line, we got out to walk past worn brownstone buildings, people grouped on door stoops, and children hopping along the curb. A couple of inches taller than me, Jayda kept her hand on my shoulder in protective ownership and I felt the old security of belonging to someone. A few people stared, but most nodded to us or called, "Hey, Sistah," to Jayda, sometimes "Mornin', Sister," to me.

"Howzitgoin'?" or "Hey, Bro," Jayda answered. I remembered a time on a Berkeley sidewalk when a woman I knew was walking briskly towards us. "Uh, oh," I had said in a low voice, "Here comes that woman, Grace. She never stops talking. I'm going to get behind you until she goes past." Jayda had stopped to glare at me.

"What is it with you white women, Mer? You don't talk to each other. You see someone coming and you hide like you're afraid."

Back in the hotel room, Jayda showered and I caught the sweet whiff of pot from behind the bathroom door. When she appeared, she was transformed in a pair of gold, wide-legged pants and a wildly colorful top of an African design we had found at a consignment shop on Telegraph Avenue. Dangling earrings gave her an unlikely feminine dazzle and a fragrant smelling oil made her skin glow. She could have been on stage with Sweet Honey.

"Hey, hey, look at you!" I admired.

"I look like a fem, that's what. A big black fem," but she was smiling. Beside her, in a plain silk blouse and black floor length skirt, I felt as boring as white bread.

Alone with our own thoughts, we were silent in the taxi up Park Avenue with its banks of red tulips down the center. Then, from Jayda, "How will I know which fork to use?" Before I could think of an answer, the taxi pulled up a circular drive to an impressive building with stone pillars and a uniformed doorman.

"Hey, Dude, whazzup?" Jayda greeted the man. This woman will never stop amazing me, I thought, and breathed a silent, "Please, God, let this be all right." Inside, we barely had time to take in the tapestry wall hangings and tiled floors before we were greeted at the ballroom door by a low bow from a gentleman wearing a kilt.

"Your names, madams?"

"Did you hear that?" Jayda hissed. "Just like in the movies." The room was filled with white tables set for eight and people talking animatedly under massive chandeliers. Waiters circulated trays of drinks, and I tried not to inhale the comforting contents of a glass of wine in a single gulp. Jayda asked for a Diet Coke. A short, balding man in a tuxedo singled us out. "I'm Richard." He stared for a long time at Jayda, perspiration beading his forehead. "You're Jayda?" He looked at me. "I thought she was..." My heart sank. It had never occurred to me to tell him Jayda was African American, not the Native American woman he had seen in the photograph. Well, I thought, we're too far into this thing now. I looked around the room hoping to see a band of "real Indians" in tribal dress, but Richard, mopping his brow with a large handkerchief, was starting to greet someone else.

"Where are the New Jersey Indians?" I asked, almost screeching in my anxiety.

"Their car broke down on the parkway. They're not coming," he said over his shoulder and was gone. I reached for another glass of wine.

"I need a cigarette," said Jayda loudly. But there wasn't time. Dinner was being announced by the gentleman in the kilt, and we found ourselves seated with six other guests at a round table near the podium. Several wine glasses graced each plate with a line of silverware on either side. An awkward silence descended on our table while we watched our waiter serve plates of delicate endive topped with smoked salmon. Jayda stared at hers, then leaned forward conversationally, both elbows on the table, to address the guests at large.

"So, here's what I want to know. I've never been to one of these dinners and I need you guys to show me which fork to use." A shadow of a pause, and then a rush of talk. Everyone wanted to help and everyone had a funny story to tell about etiquette mistakes they had once made. Jayda reached to admire a medal hanging around the neck of an official-looking gentleman next to her, his goatee bobbing as he talked. "I wish I had a medal like that," she said. Was this the same Jayda who was moodily rolling a joint in a deserted children's park only the day before?

While the roast beef was being served, Richard jumped onto the podium to give a long description of each selection of wine as it made the rounds. After my third, no, fourth glass, I decided I was having a good time. Richard was back on the podium. After an apology for the absence of the Indians who were going to dance for us, he introduced Jayda. She was, he said, a "well-known published poet from California," who had come all this way to read. At the words "well-known," I recognized with dismay the emptiness that settled over Jayda's face as she sat frozen, clutching the sheets of poems we had chosen back in Berkeley.

She leaned to me. "I can't go up there."

"Yes, you can," I hissed. She shook her head, crossed her arms stubbornly and stared at her lap.

"No."

"Yes."

"Jayda?" Richard asked from the podium.

"You can do it," I repeated. "Please, Jayda. For me." I was begging.

"Then you have to come up there too."

There was nothing else to do. Once on the small stage, I gave Jayda a push from behind, stepped back and tried to look invisible. She stood for a long moment looking at the audience and holding tight to her pages of poems. Coffee cups clinked. At last, into the microphone, a soft, "I'm Jayda." Another pause, and then with no further explanation of who she was or why she was there, she began the poem that had inspired Richard.

There once was a time
When spirits roamed free
And there was no need for houses

A quiet settled over the room.

We lived under the same skies
And our love for each other
Was as deep as canyons
Carved by all water.
My soul remembers.

When she finished, she stopped as if mesmerized, staring at the faces. "Read some more," I urged fervently from behind. Nothing.

"Thank you," she said finally, leaving me by myself as she stepped off the podium to a round of applause. Back in our seats, I didn't dare look at Richard while he closed out the program with some quip about how short speeches could be the best. If he had expected Jayda to take the place of dancers from New Jersey, he was badly disappointed. Wincing at the thought of the thousand dollars he had spent on airfare for only one poem, I jabbed a frustrated finger at the pages of poems she still clenched in one hand. I couldn't conceal my irritation. She had performed in front of plenty of audiences without losing her nerve, and I was tired of having to clean up the mood swings that left me feeling responsible.

"What happened? Why didn't you read more?"

"I don't know," she shrugged. "I guess because I didn't have your photographs next to me. That's all I could do."

Waiters served more coffee while guests came up to talk with Jayda and shake her hand. She had lost her blank look and smiled at everyone, signing her name on programs and nearly squashing the goateed official in one of her hugs. As we were leaving, I apprehensively sought out Richard to apologize for Jayda's too brief appearance, but he was nowhere to be found. In the taxi heading down Park Avenue, a wave of exhaustion and impatience with Jayda's endless drama overwhelmed me as she leaned back with a sigh. "Well, that's over. Man, I could sure use a hit."

Jayda slept all the way home on the plane while I stared out the window and tried not to think about Richard and her refusal to read. Only that morning, when I had checked out at the front registration desk, the hotel clerk had confirmed my fears. He had handed me the bill I thought would be paid by Richard. Stapled to the top was a note: *Invoice to be paid by room occupant*. Later, he never acknowledged my note of apology, and, as I expected, we never heard from him again.

Unraveling

The Sisters Project continued in high gear. In spite of my exasperation with Jayda, I owed it to our donors, our supporters and our Board to focus on performances and keep friction between Jayda and me from getting in the way. But it wasn't easy. My nerves were on edge and more than once I found myself yelling at the readers. Jayda varied between sounding like a child of God one minute and being anxiously unsure of herself the next. Then I had one of my ideas. I suggested to Jayda that she go to community college. "Remember how much you liked the high school teacher who taught you when you were homeless? What was her name? Miss Lane?" Jayda looked dubious.

"Don't make me into a project, Mer," she said.

"I'm not!" I flared. I could only imagine how thrilled she would be crossing a stage for her diploma in English to wild applause from her family. A degree would give her more confidence, and narrow the gap between us. When I offered to pay the fees, she reluctantly agreed, and the next week we went to a college near Vallejo to enroll her in an English class. She looked awkward in the low ceilinged registration office with its thick carpets and dim lights, but cheered up at a nearby Dollar Store where we bought a binder with a packet of lined paper and different colored plastic dividers. I could have been a mother outfitting my first grader at the beginning of school.

Despite her apprehension, she *did* like it, at least in the beginning. Full of enthusiasm, she called me after the first class. Mr. Bodin, the teacher, was "a cool guy" and she'd gone out for sodas with other students after class. "He likes my poetry!" she announced, and I was sure my plan was going to work. But in a few weeks, her ardor began to fade. Her tone was flat when she told me that Mr. Bodin wanted to send some of her poems to the school newspaper.

"That's wonderful, Jayda," I insisted. "Your writing is going to be recognized!"

"I dunno." She didn't want to write poetry any more, she said. She had no muse. Before long she was cutting classes either without telling me or making excuses. "I'm a loser, Mer. I've always been a loser." Nothing I said could make a difference, and I couldn't understand it when after a while she stopped going to school at all. It didn't occur to me that doing well in a classroom might be scary for her, that once she had succeeded, she would have to go on succeeding. I couldn't admit I was trying to turn her into someone she didn't want to be.

Lawanda and Mona were getting married. Everyone was going. I thought of staying home, but it was my first lesbian wedding and I wanted to know what they would wear and what they would be called. The bride and groom? The bride and bride? When I arrived at the community center, Mona had pulled out all the stops with a voluminous white gown, satin pumps and a sparkling tiara. Lawanda grinned self-consciously in a rented tuxedo, and Jayda, in a matching tuxedo, seemed excited to be Lawanda's best man. Her eyes were bright and she was in such high spirits that I hung back, feeling apprehensive at her mood and wishing I hadn't promised Lawanda I would come. After the ceremony, while a professional DJ warmed up on the stage, Jayda found me at the back of the room, put her arm around me and pulled me close. "You know what I'm going to do? I'm going to go up on that stage and tell everyone me and you are getting married."

"You're going to do *what?*" I pulled away, thinking at first she was teasing, but looking at her determined expression gave me a feeling of dread that made my skin prickle. Immersed in the progress of our work and our unique bond, I had avoided thinking about the future. Clearly, she believed there was more to it than was possible. But now my only thought was to keep her from going on the stage.

"You're not doing any such thing," I said, wanting to keep my tone light, as if she were only making a joke.

"I mean it," she said, with a sudden manic laugh.

"You can't do that, Jayda." I had to make her understand. "We aren't that way, okay?" I softened my voice. "We're really good friends, but we're too different. We need to talk about this. I need to explain. We can't ever get married." I reached to hold her arm, but stiff with hurt, Jayda backed away, her face stricken. I watched her elbow her way into a group of Lawanda's friends who were passing out cigarettes, and disappear through the back door to smoke. Rigid with worry about Jayda and disappointment in myself, I found my car in the parking lot and drove myself home.

When Jayda told me the next week she had gone back to using crack, it was hard to hear. But when I stopped to think about it, it wasn't a surprise. Friends told me later that her first relapse had happened months before, and I berated myself that I hadn't picked up on it. Of course it made sense—her jumpiness in New York, her mood swings, the way she kept disappearing, the way she always came up broke. "The bank made a mistake," she would protest, shamefaced and distant looking. Or, "My tax rebate will be here next week and then I'll pay you back." Tangled in confusion and guilt, I always bailed her out.

Lawanda tried to warn me. "Listen, Mer. Jayda's got wounds that go so far back they aren't ever going to heal. You're not doing her any good. You gotta learn to say no." But I didn't listen. I didn't know how to stop loaning Jayda money and supporting her in any way I could. She agreed to enroll in the outpatient program at Kaiser, and thirty days later announced she was clean. And meant it. To celebrate, I took her to Nation's for a cheeseburger and fries. But nothing lasts with crack except uncertainty. Months blended together in a constantly shifting pattern of relapse and recovery. When she told me she'd been to crack houses, I was shocked trying to imagine what those places must be like. Could the loving and gentle woman I thought I knew sit stupefied for days among drug dealers and trash? We went on doing a few performances with the Sisters Project, but my anxiety was now so chronic I hardly noticed it any more.

If our friends on the Board knew Jayda was using crack, they didn't say so and neither did I. She could show up at a Sisters meeting looking as normal as apple pie and making suggestions for a fundraiser, and the next week be hospitalized for suicidal depression. "This place would bring depression on for any one," I said, on one of my visits to the ward's bare meeting area with its handful of tired magazines and the one phone that was constantly in use. She smiled, but as I left and the door closed behind me, her face through the window was a moon of despair.

Lawanda tried again. "You need to go to Nar-Anon," she told me without equivocation. Finally, I agreed to go to one meeting for families and friends of addicts. "Just this once," I said.

"This is all Jayda's fault," I complained to myself, uncomfortable and resentful, as I drove one evening through endless stoplights to the other side of Oakland. But I knew in my heart that wasn't true. In a small room on Sutter Hospital's 5th floor, I joined a miscellaneous handful of people who sat around a table and read long lists of steps and traditions and told stories about how they struggled to say no to the addicts in their lives.

"Keep coming back," they told me at the end of the meeting. Not on your life, I thought, but Lawanda's words stayed with me, *You're not doing her any good. You gotta learn to say no.* The next week I went back. Gradually, I began to find comfort in this diverse little group, in its repetition of the readings and affirmations. The stories made sense, and over time, I even summoned the courage to tell a couple of my own.

My efforts to keep the Sisters Project performances going were not a success. At one disastrous campus radio session, the interviewer was bewildered and I was chagrined when Jayda's words came out garbled or not at all. Citing stress and fatigue, I told the Board we needed a break, and they agreed the Project should be put on hold.

But it wasn't over. Not yet. My friend and skilled videographer, Hannah, wanted to use our performance as the basis for a filmed documentary about homeless women and children. We began to meet once a week, and I thrived on our meticulous work and her relentless attention to every detail.

Jayda's relapses had become less frequent, but we were rarely together now except when she was stable enough to hang out in a corner of Hannah's office, hands resting across her belly, sometimes drowsy, other times alert. She made occasional suggestions and teased us about the detailed precision of our work. "Don't ever hang a show with Mer," she said to Hannah, with a grin. "If a photo is a quarter inch off, she's going to make you move it." It took nearly a year, but when we were finished, Jayda and I had a video that we could now use in place of a live show.

Deep Wounds

A therapist once told me that people die the way they live.
I believe that to be true.

One evening I called Jayda to remind her of the meeting I had scheduled the next day to discuss showing the video at the College of Arts in Oakland. Our voices had been soft, wrapped in bunting, careful not to hurt each other.

"Hey, how's it going?" I asked. "Are you okay?"

A muted, "I'm okay. My back's been real bad though. I took some of those pain pills."

"How many did you take?"

"I don't know."

"What else? Have you been taking anything else?"

"Nothin'."

"I can't hear you. You're sure?"

"I'm sure."

"You'll be there then?" We hadn't seen each other for several weeks. I pictured how she would look on the bench in front of the apartments where she lived with a woman I barely knew, her body wide, her face alight at the sight of my car. "Ten o'clock, okay? Our meeting is at 10:30. Don't forget." I was getting ready for bed when the phone rang. It was Jayda again.

"Mer, I just want to tell you." There was a long pause. "I love you."

"I love you too, Jay. Are you sure you're okay?"

"Yeh. I'm okay," and she hung up.

A traffic light on San Pablo took forever to change, and impatient, my fingers drummed against the steering wheel. I shifted in my seat, restless with a vague sense of foreboding. Jayda usually called me the morning of an appointment to tell me that she'd be waiting, but this time there had been no call. I pulled out my phone to check for messages, punched in the code and listened to my machine voice that always sounded as if I had forgotten how to breathe. There was one message, but it wasn't Jayda. Someone cleared her throat, and then there was a voice that sounded like a woman reading a script. "This is the supervisor at Hillview Apartments. I am calling to inform you that Jayda Jackson has expired."

Expired? The word was ludicrous in its old fashioned formality. People don't expire. Food expires. Leases expire. The car behind me honked. Stupefied with fear and disbelief, I pulled over to the curb to listen to the message again. There was that word. *Expired.* It can't be true.

Do something, I told myself, always my first reaction to catastrophic news. Tell someone. Call someone. Lawanda needs to know. Oh, God, that woman at the College of Arts. I've got to call her. She needs to know. "I'm sorry," I said when she answered. "We can't make our appointment this morning."

"You do know, it's in fifteen minutes?" she said, clearly impatient. We had messed up her morning.

"I know. Something has happened." We certainly have an excuse, I thought suddenly, and felt hysterical laughter well up inside me as if this were some kind of a joke. It was the type of craziness Jayda would have loved. There was a pause while I tried to push out the words. "Jayda has died." Without waiting for her reply, I clicked the phone shut.

Expired. Expired. Expired. I left a message on Lawanda's phone and steered the car towards the apartment building where, past the bus bench, a paramedic truck waited, revolving light still on. Then it was true. Expired. Was I always going to learn about death from an answering machine? Inside the building, someone pointed to an elevator. I took the stairs. Outside Jayda's room, a policeman held up his hand, but I brushed past him, barely noticing Jayda's housemate who stared blankly at Jayda from a corner chair.

Jayda lay flat on her back on the floor, her eyes closed. A grey blanket covered her mountainous abdomen and was pulled to her chin as if she had complained of the cold. A tube stuck of out of her mouth and her skin was tinged a yellow-grey. Where were the paramedics? Had they gone out for coffee? I sank down by her head to stroke her face, my softly repeated, "Oh, oh, oh" the only sound in the room. Every detail around us was vivid—the unraveled edge of the cheap Oriental rug, the overhead light left on, a ragged plant drooping off the window sill. What must that cop in the doorway be thinking about two white women sitting silent vigil next to the body of a large black woman on the floor? I almost smiled knowing that Jayda would have smiled too.

Suddenly through the open window, there was a squeal of tires and voices yelling. I scrambled up in time to see Lawanda's car pull in behind the paramedic truck, its doors fly open and women pile into the street. Tina was the loudest, screaming over the others. I watched them disappear into the entrance of the building and heard their wails float up the stairs, down the hall towards me and into the room. Tina threw herself onto Jayda with one howl of grief-stricken rage and beat on her chest with her fists. "Stop it, Jayda! Get up!" She yelled. "Don't do this to us, Jayda. Get up!" Sobbing, Patricia stood over her, and Mona, her face tear-stained, hovered behind Lawanda and Brittany, who were trying to pull Tina away. No one paid attention to me on the floor in the middle of the raw keening that filled the room.

I have to get out of here, I thought suddenly, surprising myself by my abruptness. I knew as surely as I had ever known anything that I had to leave. These women, I thought, these women I love, they need to be alone with Jayda, to grieve in their own way. She belongs to them. She has never belonged to me. They are her tribe, her family, her world. I held her face for a moment between my hands and kissed her forehead just as

Tina broke away from Lawanda and fell sobbing across Jayda's chest again. I rose unsteadily to my feet as Lawanda got down to take my place. No one looked around as I tiptoed past the policeman standing guard at the door and ran down the stairs, pushed open the lobby door, and found myself standing on the sidewalk next to the empty bench. Once inside my car, the cloak of numbness fell away as I leaned my forehead onto the steering wheel and wept.

An Afterword

"Jayda came to visit me again last night," said Lawanda. "I swear to God. I sat straight up in bed 'cause I could smell cigarette smoke. Nobody in our house smokes. I'm sure it was her. I know she was down in the kitchen."

Next to our cafe table, the window was darkening in the winter afternoon. It was the first time we had seen each other for a couple of years, and looking at Lawanda across the table, I thought she looked just the same. I wondered if I did too. Whenever we saw each other, we hugged like there was no tomorrow, and over coffee we told stories about Jayda that made us laugh.

"Come on, Lawanda. Jayda couldn't still be visiting you. She's been gone now ten years."

"I know," she said. "But I swear she was there. When I went into the kitchen, I said to her, 'Girl? What you doing here? Don't you know enough to leave me alone after all these years?'" Lawanda's face was wreathed in laughter. "And that was when she left."

"Yeah, that sounds like Jayda all right," I said. "Trying to bug you like that." I could picture her in her tie-dye T-shirt settled at Lawanda's kitchen table with her pack of Kool Lights and a can of Pepsi. "You know, I'm still in touch with her family. Patricia and her other sisters, and Brittany. Even John. And I send Jayda's grandson a box of cookies every time I make a new batch. He's eighteen now. Hard to believe."

"You remember the big memorial we put on for Jayda at that community center?" Lawanda asked. "How crowded it was? Man, there were people there from all over. So many people were touched by her." We liked to talk about Jayda, but we shared family news as well. She told me that since she'd left the Drop-In, she'd taken a job in social work, and she was still looking after her elderly mom. "And you," asked Lawanda. "What are you doing? Don't tell me you're still volunteering at the Drop-In?"

"Yep, can you believe I'm still there? I'm cooking lunch once a week, same as I always did. I guess I don't know how to leave. Some of the women still come back, you know, just to say hello. It's been over twenty years since you and I first met in your office and you told me I had to volunteer." I laughed. "I'm doing a lot of photography too, and traveling to visit family. But mainly, I'm writing." I stirred my coffee. "So, Lawanda, I want to tell you. I'm writing a book, a memoir. And you're in it, and a lot of people you know from the Sisters Project."

"Well." Lawanda leaned back with her familiar, wide smile. "Now, that's a good thing. 'Cause you know what Jayda used to tell me? She used to say, *Some day, me and Mer, we're going to write a book.*"

Acknowledgments

Few writers can enjoy the luxury of an editor-in-residence. I am indebted to my daughter Kate, who has given countless hours of her time to listen, discuss, encourage, and edit the manuscript with her fine ear for nuance and eye for grammatical accuracy that have been critical to my progress. I could not have written *Out of My Shoes* without her.

I will always be grateful to Ruth Cox and Theo Cavanaugh, fellow-writers and beloved friends from the beginning, who made me write when I didn't want to, keep my drafts when I wanted to throw them away, and who helped me understand what I was trying to say.

Special thanks for the keen insights and support of my memoir-writing companion, Janette Wolf, who never failed to go the distance with me. I am indebted to Susan Moon, whose razor sharp critiques in our tutoring sessions taught me about good writing, and to Jenny Kern, fellow student, whose thoughtful comments supported me throughout.

Gratitude to my additional readers, Cynthia Clifford, Jay Gilbertson, Sandy Little, and Cam and Jenny Stout, who spent hours reading, editing and generally guiding me towards a completed manuscript. Thanks to the many friends who listened when I needed to talk, to Alison Luterman who was there for the "long haul," and to my granddaughter Kelly Stout, who believed in me when I didn't.

I will be forever grateful to everyone in the Sisters Project: the amazing readers and Board, the Advisors Group, dedicated friends and financial supporters. Their advice and willingness to hang in with us until the end made the Project possible.

Lastly, my thanks to Dillon Beach where, with life-long friends, I have spent my happiest hours walking by the water, watching the waves, and writing *Out of My Shoes*.

Author's Bio

Meredith Stout is a long-time resident of Berkeley, California. Raised in Southern California in the early 1950's, she was educated at Vassar College and married a Princeton graduate from an Upper East Side New York family. She has lived two lives: the first as a mother and traditional faculty wife, the second, after her divorce, as a photographer, writer, and social activist. In 2014, with two other authors, she published *A Basket of Words*, an anthology of twenty years of writing together, available in both paperback and audio versions. Meredith lives in North Berkeley with her daughter and two houseplants.